There are only three types of people...

Wolves. Sheep. Sheepdogs.

Which one are you? Find out here:

www.SheepdogSociety.org

CounterViolence

YOUR GUIDE TO SURVIVING A DEADLY
ENCOUNTER...AND MORE

EJ Owens

Legally Concealed Publishing
Orlando, FL

EJ Owens - Legally Concealed
3452 Lake Lynda Drive Suite 114
Orlando, FL 32817
www.legallyconcealed.org

Ordering Information:
Quantity sales. Special discounts are available on quantity purchases by corporations, associations, and others upon written request. For details, contact the Sales Department at *sales@legllyconcealed.org*.

CounterViolence/ EJ Owens—1st Edition
ISBN 978-0615914374

12345678910

Dedicated to the love of my life Jennifer
You are my inspiration and my rock!

My children: Kaleb, Olivia, and Ethan
My sunrise and my sunset, my reason for everyday
Daddy loves you!

To my Lord and Savior Jesus Christ
Yea, though I walk through the valley of the shadow of death,
I will fear no evil - Psalms 23:4

"Warriors Aren't Born. They're Made."

We Offer Real-World, Live Training Events.
For Info Go To:

www.ModernWarrior.org

MODERNWARRIOR

Introduction

For years now people have been asking me questions about shooting grips, stances, gun selection and situational tactics. Rarely, however, do people ask about the before or after mindset of a violent encounter. Nor do they show interest in the training required to be successful in those situations. Both mindset and training are as important as the grips, the gun, and the tactics.

I try, in every case, to give my elevator speech about the "why" as it applies to the "do" portion of their

question. With many people I encounter there tends to be a hint of ADHD that pokes its ugly head up during these conversations because the answer being offered to them is not so much a matter of fact as it is a matter of context.

I can answer your "do" questions, telling you "Do be sure you get this type of grip" or "Do make sure you use this type of holster and not that one", and call it a day. But, as with others, I would do you a great disservice by not sharing my elevator speech laying out the "why" and the "how" of an encounter. Some couldn't care less about this, the context of the encounter, because they envision the perfect scenario and train for it in the same predictable manner. Of course, their scenario always ends with the bad guy dying and the good guy (them) basking in victory. Others don't bask, they blink like deer in the headlights. They have that blank stare that lets me know they haven't a clue about the real world scenarios I describe.

I find it so interesting that some gun owners are content with conversation topics about tactics and gear. These are the same people that give no thought as to whom they might fight with their tactics and gear, nor do they give any thought as to the attacker's motives or the extremes to which the attacker will go to ensure their anticipated outcome actually happens.

In this book is my elevator speech—everything I want to say to those people and you! This is me telling you who you are up against so that you can practice, train, and prepare just in case you should find yourself in a deadly encounter one day. I lay out for you what evil is, how it drives the violent criminal, what can make you an easy target, and so much more. I also describe how you are going to feel emotionally should you take a life. I help you deal with it even before it happens. These are topics thatare not the hot topics at work or at parties, but, nonetheless, they need to be discussed whether you carry a weapon or not. One violent encounter will change your world or end it...forever.

It would not be possible to share insight into the violent criminal or feelings that will likely arise after an encounter without sharing a piece of me. In this book, I define for you what I stand for and what I will die for. There will be no question in your mind about me. You will need to do the same. If I were sitting right there with you, our conversation would flow pretty much like this book. So as you read it, hear me, talk back to me, argue with me, learn from me. With this book in your hands it is as though I was there with you.

I wrote the chapter titled *A Hero's Death* just for you. I can't express how emotional this chapter was for me as it sets forth who I am and whom I continually strive to be. To see these words on a page sharing my deepest heart-felt feelings and mind-based commitments is truly emotional. So, if when you read this, you happen to shed a few tears like I did when I wrote it, you're fine! Just quickly dry them before someone sees you.

I hope that after you finish this book you will pass it on to your friends and encourage them to read it as well. Then, compare notes and see how it made them feel. Let me know about it. You can email me at ejowens@legallyconcealed.org. I, personally, will respond to you.

Let me close with this: What is in this book is what I share with all my students. I have even more that I discuss with my friends. I hope that we will meet one day soon and continue this conversation in person. Until then, *Stay Alert and Practice Often!*

Are You A Sheep Or Sheepdog?
Find out here:
www.SheepdogSociety.org

Contents

In violence, we forget who we are.

—Mary McCarthy, Author

Your FREE Gift Is Waiting For You Here:

www.SheepdogSociety.org

CHAPTER 1

Violence

Definition:

vi·o·lence \ˈvī-lən(t)s, ˈvī-ə-\

n.

: the use of physical force to harm someone, to damage property, etc.

: great destructive force or energy

When we hear the word *violence* horrible pictures come to mind. The vast array of movies we watch contain more extravagant methods of violence than most of us are able to comprehend. Unlike the violence we watch on TV, actual violence we encounter will not have the hard-hitting, fast-paced music playing over our heads nor will it have the off-angle, slow-motion camera shot of us as the hero boldly and successfully fighting the bad guy. More than likely the violence we encounter will be sudden, fast, and very scary.

Violence, though, can take on many different forms and we must be able to recognize them for what they are. In our daily lives, we rarely encounter violence so we are not prepared to deal with it physically or emotionally. When the very few of us do actually encounter violence, we tend to stand in disbelief, even if for only for a moment, that it is actually happening. I want to shape for you some types of violence you might encounter should it decide that you would be the next victim. As we look at violence, strive to understand that type of violence at its worst. Doing so will give you a better understanding of what will be needed from you in order to survive.

TYPES OF VIOLENCE

PHYSICAL VIOLENCE

Aggression may be physical or verbal. Verbal aggression is not considered violent. Physical aggression is not necessarily violent although research studies show that it is an act intended to cause harm, but not death, to the recipient. Physical aggression becomes *physical violence* when the act gains the intention of causing harm to the recipient with death as an acceptable outcome. Physical violence often involves the use of bats, crowbars, knives, guns or even someone's bare hands with the intent to "harm unto death". As we will discuss later on, intent is immensely important in our judicial system.

Anger is a frequent stimulus of aggressive behavior, just as aggression can result from intoxication or frustration. Aggressive behavior may result from medical conditions. People suffering from advanced Alzheimer's disease, for example, may manifest aggression due to diminished cognitive capacity, confusion or frustration according to many studies on this disease. Injured athletes, wounded soldiers, disabled car crash victims, and even cancer patients may demonstrate aggressive behavior. Self-mutilation (physical aggression turned against oneself) often occurs in conjunction with serious mental disorders, such as borderline personality disorder Not often, however, does this aggressive behavior turn into violent.

According to studies of violent criminals in particular, physical violence is an act of will manifested as a deliberate action intended to harm another, even to the point of death. Guns, knives, swords, even bombs, in and of themselves are not violent as they have no mind or will and therefore cannot choose to act. They are merely tools through which a person can cause physical harm to another.

Should you encounter violence, you will most assuredly encounter physical violence.

VERBAL HOSTILITY
The child's taunt "sticks and stones may break my bones but words will never hurt me" seldom prevents the emotional distress that verbal lashes often provide. Emo-

tional distress may become emotional abuse as verbal lashes become frequent and drawn out. Verbal lashes or outcries then become *verbal hostility.*

Verbal hostility (sometimes called *verbal harassment* or *verbal abuse*) is manifested through negative statements made to you, made about you within your hearing range, or made about you to others. It includes behaviors such as yelling, name-calling, threatening, insulting, and bullying through words.

So significant is the impact of verbal hostility, the Mayo Clinic includes name-calling and insults under the category of *domestic violence.* Psychologists remind parents that simple put-downs—whether intentional or perceived—can have profound detrimental effects on their children, their aged parents, or other family members. For children, the detrimental effects may continue into adulthood and possibly give way to physical violence.

Should you encounter violence, you will most likely encounter verbal hostility.

NONVERBAL INTIMIDATION
Nonverbal intimidation often implies the threat of violence, at least in the perception of the person on the receiving end. Stalking, for example, involves one or more forms of nonverbal intimidation, such as following the victim, planting malicious software in a victim's computer, sending unwanted gifts and vandalizing the victim's property. A well-known example of nonverbal intimidation occurred during the movie "Fatal Attraction" when Alex kills her victim's daughter's pet rabbit.

Should you encounter violence, you are likely to experience some type of nonverbal intimidation.

PASSIVE AGGRESSIVE BEHAVIOR

The Mayo Clinic defines *passive aggressive behavior* as an indirect way of expressing displeasure or anger. I define it as simply "aggression in passive behavior clothing." Often spurred from extreme resentment, the passive aggressive lacks the willingness or the ability to express this resentment directly. This behavior may demonstrate itself through the withholding of something you need. The withholding is a form of punishment.

The passive aggressive will rarely say what they mean or mean what they say. They act only after they cause you some kind of stress, usually through poor or ambiguous communication. Often, they will agree to perform a task (like putting down their weapon when ordered), but will procrastinate in their performance of the agreed action or deliberately perform a different action as manifestation of anger or out of a desire to perform harm to someone else.

If you become a victim, passive aggressive behavior may seem logical at the time, but you may find that such behavior antagonizes the criminal. Use it if it works to buy time or serves as a distraction, but avoid it if it doesn't work.

Should you encounter violence, you are likely to find yourself utilizing passive aggression as the victim or to have the criminal use this behavior as a means to control you by promising something you want or need, but failing to provide it.

TYPES OF VIOLENT CRIME

Nearly every state classifies a crime as either a "felony" or a "misdemeanor." A felony crime usually involves potential or real harm against a human life or property. Although state laws may not all agree, crimes typically considered as felonies include kidnapping, murder, arson, and criminal assault. A misdemeanor is a less serious crime and again varies from state to state. Typically, misdemeanors include shoplifting, trespassing, indecent exposure, and public intoxication among others.

The *Federal Bureau of Investigation's Uniform Crime Report* (FBI UCR) identifies four categories of crime as violent crimes and in nearly every state, these crimes are felonies:

1. Murder

2. Forcible rape

3. Robbery

4. Aggravated Assault

Let's look at what defines each of these crimes.

MURDER

Murder is the taking of another's life with "malice aforethought" (the intention to kill). Manslaughter differs from murder in that there no obvious intention to kill as in vehicular manslaughter, which may occur during a car accident. To help the legal system remain as fair as possible, the law actually categorizes murder in several different ways. One category used by some states is felony murder, which is a murder committed during the act of another felony crime. In other states, felony murder falls under the category of first-degree murder.

No matter if your state recognizes felony murder as a crime separate and distinct from first-degree murder or not, felony murder is a very serious charge that can have permanent repercussions on the murderer's life. If convicted of felony murder, you will have to face jail time and other serious penalties to include the death penalty.

TYPES OF FELONIES ASSOCIATED WITH MURDER

First degree murder may or may not be associated with another felony. Felony murder occurs during the course of another felony. In addition to the four felonies already names, nearly every state recognizes these acts as felonies:

- ☑ Burglary

- ☑ Arson

- ☑ Kidnapping

Even accidental deaths can count as felony murders in some states. For example, if you are burglarizing the home owner's upstairs bedroom and the owners walk in, they may turn to run down the stairs after seeing you. If one of the owners slips while running down the stairs, falls to the bottom and dies, you (the robber) will likely be held accountable for the owner's death as well as the robbery.

FORCIBLE RAPE

Rape is a type of sexual assault usually involving sexual intercourse initiated by one or more persons against another person without that person's consent. *Forcible rape* is be carried out by physical force, coercion, abuse of authority or against a person who is incapable of valid consent, such as one who is unconscious, incapacitated, or below the legal age of consent.

Rape may leave the victim, whether male or female, severely traumatized even to the point of suffering from post traumatic stress disorder (PTSD). In addition to psychological harm resulting from the act, rape may cause physical injury or leave behind a sexually transmitted infection or a pregnancy. Following a rape, a victim may face further violence or threats of violence from the rapist if he or she is not caught and prosecuted.

ROBBERY

Robbery is the crime of taking or attempting to take something of value by force or threat of force or by putting the victim in fear. Robbery differentiates itself from other forms of theft (such as burglary, shoplifting or car theft) by its inherently violent nature. Whereas many lesser forms of theft are punished as misdemeanors, robbery is always a felony crime for this reason.

Types of robbery include *armed robbery* when a firearm is involve, *aggravated robbery* when a deadly weapon is involved and *highway robbery*, which involves a mugging in a public place such as a sidewalk or street. *Carjacking* is a form of robbery as is *extortion*, which uses words instead of actions to accomplish the theft.

AGGRAVATED ASSAULT

An assault is an intentional act by one person that creates the threat of an imminent harmful contact. In most jurisdictions, *aggravated assault* is the attempt to cause serious bodily injury to another person on purpose, knowingly or recklessly by using a deadly weapon. A person commits an aggravated assault when that person:

- causes serious bodily injury to another person with a deadly weapon

- performs assaults in the victim's home (in most states)

- causes grievous bodily harm to another person, such as with rape or kidnapping

- has sexual relations with a person who is under the age of consent

- causes bodily harm by recklessly operating a motor vehicle

Now that you realize crimes like those you see in *Law and Order* and *CSI* can and do happen-and they are sometimes as violent as the shows portray, let's look at violent crimes from the victim's perspective. Crimes with violence, either real or threatened, require that you as the victim defend yourself physically. It may also require that you wound or take the life of your attacker. This act is called *self-defense*.

> *If someone shouts "I'm going to kill you!" you should...no, you must believe that they mean what they say and take whatever action you feel is appropriate under the circumstances.* Self-defense websites

RIGHT OF SELF-DEFENSE

The *right of self-defense* according to U.S. law is the right for U.S. citizens acting on their own behalf to engage in a level of violence, called "reasonable force" or "defensive force." The law recognizes reasonable force, including the use of deadly force against someone else, whenever you do so to defend one's own life or the lives of others.

> *"Guns are used up to 2.5 million times each year in self-defense in the United States". -"The Armed Citizen": America's 1st Freedom, National Rifle Association, March 2013*

It is important to understand...

When the bad guy is no longer a threat (e.g. by being tackled and restrained, surrendering, or fleeing) the justification of self-defense will fail if you continue to attack or to punish beyond imposing physical restraint.

Let's say you are at some location other than your house and taunted to fight. If you accept the challenge instead of walking away, and to end it, you use deadly force, don't bother to tell the judge, "I was only defending myself." You will likely see the judge laugh to himself! That's how unlikely your justification will save you from prosecution.

The same is true if you use force and declare that you were protecting someone else from danger as your justification. You must have a reasonable belief that the "someone else" is in a position where he or she would have the right of self-defense *before* using force—and be able to convince the cops that your belief was correct.

JUSTIFIABLE HOMICIDE

To be considered "justified," a homicide must show that it was committed to prevent a very serious crime, such as murder, rape or armed robbery. The bad guy's intent to commit a serious crime must be clear at the time of the homicide. Conversely, a homicide performed out of vengeance or retribution for action in the past is unlikely to be considered justifiable. The FBI UCR Program defines and limits *justifiable homicide* to:

★ The killing of a felon by a police officer in the line of duty

★ The killing of a felon by a private citizen during the commission of a felony

When looking for similarities and differences among 277 recent justifiable homicides, the FBI found that 230 (83%) of the homicides resulted from a firearm. Of the 230 homicide victims:

✓ 82 (35.7 %) were known to the private citizen who used the firearm *including acquaintance, boyfriend, brother, common-law husband, employee, ex-husband, ex-wife, father, friend, girlfriend, husband, in-law, neighbor, other family, other known, son, step-father, stepson, and wife*

✓ 130 (56.5 %) were strangers

✓ 18 (07.8 %) the relationship was unknown

Of the 230 justifiable homicides resulting from a firearm:

- 205 (89.1%) were committed by men
- 24 (10.4%) were committed by women
- 1 (0.4%) the shooter's gender was unknown

Of the 230 firearms used in the justifiable homicides:

- 166 (72.2%) were handguns
- 28 (12.2 %) were shotguns
- 8 (03.5 %) were rifles
- 28 (12.2 %) were firearms, type not stated

Self-defense is an acceptable defense within our judicial system. It is not difficult to prove under most circumstances, especially when the incident happens in your own home and the other party is unknown to you. Although you may spend some time in a police station after the incident, that is a small price to pay for your life and those of your loved ones or friends.

CASTLE DOCTRINE

The *Castle Doctrine* (or the *Defense of Habitation Law*), is enacted in 24 states listed in Appendix A as of this publishing. The Castle Doctrine argues that one cannot be expected to retreat from one's own home - a man's house is his castle, *et domus sua cuique est tutissimum refugium*," which is Latin for "and one's home is the safest refuge."

Checking the list in Appendix A, you will notice that parts of the Northeast and on the Pacific Coast, there is no Castle Doctrine legislation. Not having this protection under the law requires that these homeowners retreat from their home during an active invasion instead of defending their home and property. To stay and defend their home and property puts the homeowner at risk of being prosecuted for assault or homicide and/or held liable in civil court for the criminal's medical bills or other damages the court may award.

Should a homeowner in a state with no Castle legislation shoot someone inside their home during an actual home invasion and the homeowner cannot prove that he or she made a concerted effort to retreat then they would, like the invader,  be charged with a crime. The thought from these states is that two wrongs don't make a right.

All right, so wrap your brain around this. A guy breaks into your home late at night. You get up and grab your wife and gun. Now what? Oh yeah, it's time for you to jump out of a window and let him finish what he started because if you can't prove you were trying to retreat and you shoot him...wait for it...YOU GO TO JAIL TOO!!!

I can only pray that if you live in a state without an enacted Castle Doctrine you never have a home invasion. If you do live in a state that needs a Castle Doctrine, call your state representative and get him or her working on that legislation right now! It's for your protection that there is a law in place which allows you to defend your home and property.

When evil men plot, good men must plan.

- Martin Luther King

Modern Warrior Certification Program
No B.S. Live Gunfighting Bootcamp

You got what it takes? Apply here:

www.ModernWarrior.org

CHAPTER 2

Evil

Definition:

e·vil [ee-vuhl]

adj.
morally wrong or bad; immoral; wicked:

Evil, according to a Judeo-Christian perspective, is any action, thought or attitude that is contrary to the character of God. There is no moral action in the Bible that is contrary to the good inherent in God's character. Our founding fathers believed this and shaped our country's guiding principles to fight evil.

The strongest moral action against the good that defines God's character is to set one's self up as god. This action is belied in the attitude of *I can do what I want, how I want, when I want.* When this attitude imposes itself on others and does harm to them undeservingly, evil is at the door.

Understanding evil is easier when contrasted against morals. Morals are a set of personal values—your perception of what is right and what is wrong. Ethics deals with how one *ought* to think and act; morals are the sum of *how* you think and act. When a person acts against the expectations of the society in which he or she lives, society considers those actions evil.

Let me stop here and share with you this thought. Hopefully, it will broaden your point-of-view some. Muslims *(those which we in America call "radical Muslims")* following their interpretation of the Qur'an, believe that God (Allah) dictates to them the necessity of ultimately killing all non-believers of Islam. This purification, they say, will bring society back to a oneness that worships only "The One True God." Based on this belief, their morals allow killing others for this reason without defining it as murder. Chinese morals do not value human life above the good of the government. American society, however, treats murder as immoral—even evil—as murder is outside the good defined by God's character. American society, generally speaking, also accepts the act of killing another to preserve one's own life or the lives of others as morally acceptable, believing that is how God would react and therefore, not evil.

Looking only at the act of killing can be misleading. Just as "God looks at the heart" we say, we must also look at the intent of the person performing the act. Consider this: A woman is stopped for speeding on the interstate. Was she breaking the law? Yes! When the officer approaches the car he finds that the mother is rushing her daughter, who is actively having an asthma attack, to the hospital. In this case, the officer changes his perspective. Instead of writing the mother a speeding ticket, he moves quickly to meet the emergency needs of the daughter. Intent is key! Just as the Bible tells us that God looks not so much as to what we do, but as to why we do it, the American judicial system, created by our forefathers as a part of a Judeo-Christian society, looks closely at intent before determining that some action is a crime.

Here is something else for you to ponder. When tragedy happens invariably the question of "why" comes up—"Why did he kill those innocent people?" or "Why did that car accident happen?" It is the "why" that forces us to consider intent. Although we do not want to forget the "who", in the end it is the "why" that is most important. When we find out the "who" and the "why" we begin the process of holding someone or some people accountable. The point here is that evil defines intent more so than the actual act. It speaks to the reasoning one had even before his or her actions.

There are many acts that our society considers as criminal, yet many criminals are not evil. They have broken laws set by society, but their actions were without intent to impose harm on others in the process. There are criminals who have broken laws relative to abusing prescription drugs, not paying taxes, or writing bad checks. Without the intent to harm others for their own personal gain, as in the case of these crimes, society does not consider these crimes "heinous" or "evil".

In the act of protecting one's home and/or loved ones, even strangers and their property, without the intent for personal gain, there is no evil at work. What is at work is what I call *CounterViolence*.

Countering violence aimed at you, your loved ones, or even strangers was recognized by our forefathers as a probability, a possibility, a necessity. They then insured that America's people could counter violence with the full permission of the Federal Government through the Second Amendment with the right to bear arms. Even with recent legislation of both the Federal government and state governments to curtail the recognition and intent of those who ratified our constitution, our constitution continues to prevail.

There are few better measures of the concern a society has for its individual members and its own well being than the way it handles criminals.

-Ramsey Clark, former U.S. Attorney General

Sheep or Sheepdog
Which One Are You?
Find Out Now. Go To:
www.SheepdogSociety.org

CHAPTER 3

Criminals

Definition:

crim·i·nal (kr m -n l)

n.
:One that has committed or been legally convicted of a crime.
adj.
:Of, involving, or having the nature of crime: criminal abuse.

It is possible that a person can commit acts considered "evil" without ever being labeled a criminal by our society. Most things our society considers evil, however, would in fact be a crime should the offending person be caught and subsequently convicted. Should someone bring violence to your doorstep, I want you to be able to size up that person and make some sound conclusions about that person's intentions and probable actions.

Even after centuries of study by researchers in countries around the world, the physical, psychiatric (mental), and psychological (behavioral) make-up of criminals continues to be studied to find some predisposition that would lead them to do such acts. Theories about criminal behavior abound. Cesare Lombroso, an Italian criminologist, argued in 1876 that criminals are born as criminals. His research led to later studies of why one twin becomes a criminal when the other does not. Based on his research in the late 1800's, today's technologies allow researchers to study neurophysiological conditions as they attempt to predefine criminals. The now-popular explanation for childhood behavioral issues, ADHD, sometimes serves as an explanation for criminal behavior.

Freud laid the groundwork around the turn of the twentieth century for studies on the effect of childhood traumatic events and family events as the instigator of criminal behavior. In 1939, Edwin Sutherland claimed that criminal behavior is learned, just as any other learning takes place. Albert Bandura set forth an explanation for criminal behavior in 1976 that associates a person's observational learning in the family, close surroundings, and through books and television with likely criminal behavior. *Eysenck's Personality Theory* of the late 1970s proposes that extroverts are more likely to participate in criminal behavior than introverts.

Researchers in the 1970s sought to blame society rather than the individual for his or her criminal behavior. Based on Marxist principles, the theory of *Radical*

Criminology was born. This theory purports the idea that no act is naturally immoral or criminal. Instead, it explains the "immoral" or "criminal" act performed as action responding to the economic and societal forces of a society. The theory sees the justice system as existing primarily to serve the wealthy and oppress the poor.

The Strain Theory, on the other hand, proposes that poor people commit crime because it is their only way to get ahead. It excuses criminal behaviors of the poor arguing that poor people commit crimes because they can't help themselves.

Theories are plentiful and support most any point-of-view. As the reader, you decide what you think influences a person, poor or wealthy, to commit a crime. This decision is one of the most important you will make because it will predetermine your position on countering violence that may seek to hurt you, your loved ones, your friends, or even strangers near you. Before you make your decision, however, let's look at a few crime theories in greater detail.

INDIVIDUAL CRIME THEORY

The *individual crime theory group* is broken down into three separate categories: psychological, psychiatric and physical. We will look at each of these.

PSYCHOLOGICAL
Psychological explanations for criminal behavior include:

1. The criminal has a personality that was predisposed by some environmental action which prompted an internal response from the criminal to commit the crime.

2. The criminal lacks intelligence or mental ability that would enable him or her to have better opportunities to reach personal goals in a legitimate way or to adjust better socially.

3. The criminal cannot process information the way others do. This inability leads the criminal to resort to behaviors others would not even attempt due to his or her different thought patterns

4. The criminal has character defects due to brain damage or extensive mistreatment at home.

PSYCHIATRIC

Psychiatric explanations for criminal behavior include:

1. The criminal never fully developed all aspects of his or her personality in a healthy and normal way and, thereby, he or she is stuck in an immature state.

This explanation points towards criminals being unable to deny themselves an impulse. This ability to deny impulses, in turn, impairs the criminal's abilities to understand why they do what they do.

2. The criminal inherited his or her criminality through biology—through genes handed off to him or her by at least one of the biological parents.

PHYSICAL

Physical explanations for criminal behavior include:

1. The criminal has a chemical imbalance of some sort in the body.

2. The criminal has a hormonal imbalance.

Throughout history, criminologists have looked to a wide range of factors to explain why a person commits crimes. They have considered biological or genetic factors, psychological factors, physical factors and even social and economic factors. Yet, there is still no consensus on the cause of criminal behavior.

Long-term research studies and on-going research indicate that, most often, a combination of factors bring a person to commit a crime. At some point, however, the criminal must take responsibility for his or her actions. Our justice system strives to ensure that such responsibility is taken.

REASONS

Reasons for committing a crime span elements such as greed, anger, jealously, revenge, pride, personal satisfaction or a sense of accomplishment. Some criminals decide to commit a crime by setting a goal and carefully planning all details in advance to increase gain and decrease risk. They derive great joy from planning and executing the event according to that plan. Others get an adrenaline rush when carrying out a dangerous crime successfully, so they plan to ensure execution, but not for the joy of planning. From their point-of-view, planning is a requirement. It is work! Planning for whatever reason causes the criminal to make choices about his or her behavior. Thus, the criminal demonstrates intent. Still others commit crimes on impulse, or out of rage or fear.

The desire for material gains (money or belongings) leads to property crimes like robbery, burglary, auto theft, and white-collar crimes such as embezzlement, extortion, identity theft, bribery and others. Property crimes, nearly always planned in advance, have the criminal's end focus on the item desired.

A driving desire for control, revenge, or power typically leads to violent crimes such as murders, assaults, and rapes. The desire may cause the potential criminal to plan the crime or it may surge within the potential criminal leading to action on impulse. This is usually the case when emotions run high.

It is argued by some criminologists that domestic factors play a significant role in shaping criminal behavior. Policymakers at last are coming to recognize the connection between the breakdown of the family and various social problems. Welfare reform advocates base their agenda on research that shows children born into single parent families are much more likely to fall into poverty and welfare dependence in later years than are children with two parents in the home.

Children today do face a daunting array of problems including cheating, bullying, drugs, teenage sex, too little money and even too much money. How they choose to handle their problems is learned largely from observing older siblings, parents or guardians in the home and extended family outside the home. Whether from a single-parent home or a two-parent home, research shows a child's problems left unnoticed or ignored can manifest themselves through acts of property crime, violent acts toward another person not ending in death, and even murder.

These descriptions are quite general and somewhat overlap. That is my point. Human behavior is volatile and an inexact science. If someone close to you commits a crime, there is no need to sit for hours to "point my finger to just exactly why he/she did that." The "why" probably has more to do with his/her "want to" than anything else other than a recognized medical issue. A person's "want to" leads to planned crime just as it leads to "in the moment" crime. When I pull a gun on someone threatening my life or the lives of those around me, I believe that the person "wants to" harm me making me "want to" stop him from doing so.

EVIDENCE

A review of the empirical evidence in the professional literature of the social sciences gives us an insight into the probable root causes of crime. Consider, for instance:

- Over the past thirty years, the rise in violent crime parallels the rise in families abandoned by fathers.

- State-by-state analysis by Heritage scholars indicates that a 10% increase in the percentage of children living in single parent homes leads typically to a 17% increase in juvenile crime.

- The type of aggression and hostility demonstrated by a future criminal often is foreshadowed in unusual aggressiveness as early as age five or six.

- The future criminal tends to be an individual rejected by other children as early as the first grade and goes on to form his own group of friends, often the future delinquent gang.

On the other hand:

- Neighborhoods with a high degree of religious practice are not high crime neighborhoods.

- Over 90% of children from safe, stable homes do not become delinquents. By contrast only 10% of children from unsafe, unstable homes avoid crime.

- Criminals capable of sustaining marriage gradually move away from a life of crime after they get married.

- The mother's strong affectionate attachment to her child is the child's best buffer against a life of crime.

- The father's authority and involvement in raising his children is also a substantial and effective buffer against a life of crime.

The scholarly evidence, in short, suggests that at the heart of the explosion of crime in America is the loss of the capacity of fathers and mothers to be responsible in caring for the children they bring into the world. This loss of love and responsibility at the intimate levels of marriage and family has broad social consequences for children and for the greater community. The empirical evidence shows that too many young men and women from broken families tend to have a much weaker sense of connection with their neighborhood and are prone to exploit its members to satisfy their unmet needs or desires. This contributes to a loss of a sense of community and to the disintegration of neighborhoods into social chaos and violent crime.

So you see, on one hand we have criminal acts that, arguably, have external influential effects that drive persons to commit crime while thus attempting to change to person's physical environment. On the other hand, we have heinous acts intended to bring about change in the person's emotional environment.

HEINOUS ACTS

Definition:

hei·nous [heynuhs]

adj. hateful; odious; abominable; totally reprehensible: a heinous offense.

Heinous acts are those that are deliberate in a way to cause or to contribute to lasting harm to others. They are extreme and unforgiveable by our current society. In our everyday life we rarely encounter a true heinous act, but when we do it is even more rare to actually survive if that act is directed at us. Once we know what a heinous act of violence really is, only then can we understand what is truly needed to counter that violence and survive.

I have talked about bringing "enough force to bear" to defeat an evil act in my DVDs and online articles (also can be found at *www.legallyconcealed.org*), but this is something worth repeating. You must defend yourself from heinous types of violence with enough counterviolence to defeat it. Most of us are not willing to discuss openly that such a crime could happen to us or one of our loved ones, much less be prepared to enact *CounterViolence* should we meet violence.

There are three types of heinous acts of violence that we need to be aware of so that if someday we come face-to-face with one of them we understand the criminal's mindset and what will be required of us to prevail:

1. Serial Killer

2. Mass Murderer

3. Rapist

SERIAL KILLER
There are a lot of questions posed at this juncture, so let's pause briefly and take a look at some facts beginning

with the commonly accepted definition of the term serial killer.

The *FBI Behavioral Science Unit* (now the *Investigative Support Unit*) in Quantico, Virginia identifies a serial killer as a person who:

- Kills three or more victims *(most often one victim at a time)*

- Kills over a period of time, usually days, weeks, months or years

- Takes a cooling off period between killings

It is this latter point - the cooling off period - that separates a serial killer from a mass murderer. Ted Bundy, Jeffrey Dahmer, and Robert Ledd Yates are easily recalled serial killers. Their killings were spread over years with long cooling off periods.

MASS MURDERER

The current sprees of mass murderers suggest several different psychological characteristics in this criminal type. The first characteristic is that the potential mass murderer notices the recurrent nature of mass murders taking place in any given society. His grandiose fantasy is that he wants to out-perform past mass murderers. Therefore, this criminal diligently plans how he is going to surpass all previous mass murderers and become the greatest mass murderer in history. He becomes, in the most evil way possible, competitive towards other mass murderers. He uses his competitive and compulsive urges for murderous deeds rather than the normal competitive activities of society.

The second characteristic is that the mass murder often envies the people that he kills. He wants to die the same way that they do. With that thought, the mass murder becomes both the victim and the perpetrator of murder. He sees death as a desirable solution to his problems with the world. He may even hate the world and the people in it. He may think that he is nothing and should die along with his victims. He is a person split into parts. One part wants to kill others; the other part wishes to die. He thinks in black-and-white terms. It is either all or nothing.

A Note From EJ... It is this point alone that should encourage law enforcement officers or the concealed carrier to engage this individual immediately. By immediately engaging him you limit his rampage on others and leaving him no choice but to move to phase 2 of his plan, which is to die. At this point, this criminal is either going to be killed by you or he is going to take his own life. Either way, he will stop killing others. Get in there!

At some point the mass murderer adopts a paradoxical vision of himself as omnipotent and grandiose, and also undeserving and of little value. He rejects people and takes the position of the loner. He justifies to himself that his position is the absolute right one and dares anyone to prove that there is another way to view the world and existence.

The mass murderer is emotionally repressed, insulated and traumatically reverberating towards insults that were never resolved. He believes that he can do whatever he wants. He also believes no matter what he does, it is not going to change anything. So, he resorts to mass murder and probably suicide to change his sense of non-being...drastically. He spends years living in a black hole where part of him wants to do nothing and another part wants to do something.

When planning to mass murder, this criminal believes that he is doing something others will recognize. He experiences a feeling of being God and the devil at the

same time causing a great deal of confusion. He has the omnipotent power of life and death. His defenses make him so armored that he renders it impossible for anyone to get to him. He won't and can't feel the normal range of human emotions. A mass murderer at some point has part of his survival perception of "kill or be killed" ripped open. He proceeds to act out his fantasies onto specific and significant targets, although the targets may seem random to bystanders. It could be skin color, eye-contact, the color of the clothing, a past interaction or proximity that identifies the target. Occasionally, a mass murderer will open fire on a group with no particular stimulus from someone in the group. This action, although it seems truly random, is not random. The murderer chose that site, at that time, and therefore, those people as his targets.

Murder and suicide is the mass murderer's solution to his need to be heard, understood and accepted. His grandiosity keeps him from understanding that his very distorted thinking not only gets him rejected socially, but also alienates other people. Through mass murder and suicide, the murderer finally gets everyone's attention.

In fantasy, he gets his reckoning, but when the fantasies intensify to the point of acting out, he loses all sense of normal morality and impulse control. He doesn't question. He just acts! It is only when the mass murder commits his atrocities that people and the media start to try to analyze and understand him. In his perverse way, he has achieved his goal.

It may be easier for you to think of a mass killing incident because all of the victims are created during one event and at a single location. For example, you might remember the Columbine School incident from 1999. More recently, you might remember the Virginia Tech campus killings in 2007 or the mass killing at the Washington Navy Yard in 2013.

A *spree killing* or *rampage killing* also creates many victims like the mass murderer. The difference is that the spree killing takes place over a short period of time in more than one location, but with no "cooling of" period. The spree killer often experiences a long period of seething anger that eventually boils to a point where the killer decides to take some form of violent action. In 2000, Richard Scott Baumhammers killed 5 people during a 15-mile journey among 3 townships in Pennsylvania. In 2005, Scott Moody killed 5 within a half-mile. In 2009, Frank Garcia killed 2 at a New York hospital and hours later killed a couple in their home.

Websites such as www.massacres.us offer details of such killings.

RAPIST

The word *rape* itself originates from the Latin verb *rapere* meaning *to seize* or *take by force*. In our society, we define rape as a type of sexual assault usually involving sexual intercourse, which is initiated by one or more persons against another person without that person's consent.

Rape is not about sexual gratification; it is about control. Rapists use sexual domination of another person to make themselves feel empowered. Rapists don't consider things like getting an STD and couldn't care less if they are spreading one because for them it's not about sex. Sex is merely the vehicle to achieve the ultimate goal of empowerment.

Rapists enjoy the obedience coupled with the physical signs of grief and loss their victim is expresses. They take pleasure in afflicting emotional trauma and intimidation that they know will stay with their victim for life. Rapists revel in the fact that they have altered the emotional and physical state of that person forever. They perceive themselves as forever tied to their victim and through that they feel control. They expect some resistance. They also expect it to give way to compliance. But understand, that predators are also prepared to meet resistance with physical violence and intimidation until compliance is obtained.

The heinous criminal type just described, the rapist, expects and even demands, compliance. A rapist believes that the victim will ultimately comply when faced with intimidation and violence. What a rapist does not suspect is that you will not comply even with physical violence and intimidation, so continue to fight back. Frequently, because your consistent fighting back is unexpected, the rapist is not prepared to counter your continuing attacks.

> *"Comply and Die!"*
>
> *– EJ Owens, Legally Concealed*

The type of resistance I am referring to for a rapist and also for a serial killer or the mass murderer must be a full mind-and-body commitment to destroy that heinous individual at all costs—not just some kicking or a little screaming that stops upon the criminal's order. You must develop a mindset—determine in advance how you will react, give yourself permission to act as you have determined and then train, train, train to follow through on that determination automatically and without emotion when circumstances require it.

Guide that determination to force you to scream as loud as you can and to get your hands on him fast. Go for the eyes, ears, and throat! Put your thumbs in his eyes until you see blood and fluid oozing down your wrists. Grab the ears and pull them off if you can. If you go for the throat, grab at the rigid trachea and try to pull it out. It will seem very hard to do, but understand that the simplest act of force causes the predator to stop what he is doing to you and focus on the pain he is now experiencing. Attacking his senses is your best chance to stop his attack. Once you have a chance to break free...RUN! Run to people, lots of people, screaming and yelling as loud as you can!

There are people who are suffering beyond description. They are innocent people. They didn't bring this upon themselves. They are the victims of the sins of other people.

- Mia Farrow, Actress

In a real life or death scenario you will not, "rise to the occasion."

You will only perform at the level you've trained for.

If you want serious, tactical firearms training, I invite you to apply for the Modern Warrior Certification Program. Limited availability. Apply now:

www.ModernWarrior.org

MODERN WARRIOR

CHAPTER 4

Predatory Selection

Definition:

pred·a·tor [pred-uh-ter, -tawr]

n.
:Zoology . any organism that exists by preying upon other organisms.

:a predatory person - one who victimizes, plunders, or destroys, especially for one's own gain

:one who preys upon a weaker individual

Predators have the advantage over their prey as the predator chooses the plan, the time, the place, as well as the prey. Yet all their clever lures and traps depend upon one critical factor: the naïveté of their prey. Predators see other people as objects--objects to exploit.

Often they know they may need to kill an innocent person emotionally, if not literally, to get away with the act they want to complete. You and your life mean nothing to predators.

TYPES OF PREDATORS

FRIENDLY PREDATOR

A *friendly predator* will first try to get near his victim to isolate and trap, and then attack. A friendly predator often appeals to your sympathy by acting in need of help or needing to ask you a question about something important. Many crimes begin with a non-threatening conversation.

Not wanting to appear rude, many "soon-to-be" victims ignore their gut feelings and agree to interact with the stranger. Engaging a stranger allows the good-hearted person to become easy, naïve prey for a friendly predator.

The friendly predator is often good-looking, well dressed, charming, and acting, oh, so harmless. He may wear a uniform including a name badge, drive an official-looking vehicle, or be accompanied by a female partner. This predator may hold a baby in his arms while holding a gun in his pocket.

The lures used by friendly predators will likely surprise you—right after you are trapped. And, it will happen in the blink of an eye. Regardless of how clumsy or clever, all lures boil down to one simple warning sign:

> *He's trying to get near you to isolate you!*

FORCIBLE PREDATOR

A *forcible predator* attacks suddenly. It may be in the open or as an ambush (from some unseen position). He may first play cat-and-mouse while deciding whether or not to attack. It is nearly impossible to imagine the panic that tightens your throat or the chaos that swirls in your mind as a sudden threat forces you to make split second decisions. Yet, prudent, prior planning through understanding both your attacker and his plan will help you survive should it ever happen to you.

WHY YOU?

There are a number of reasons why a violent criminal would select you. I will generalize them by breaking them down into two simple categories: *Physical Traits* and *Environmental Situations.*

A few key physical traits that are more susceptible to victimization than most include:

Lack of confidence – Failing to project confidence in all that you do gives a predator a perception that you would be unwilling to resist his move on you. This perception in the mind of the violent attacker makes you an easy target.

> *A Note From EJ...You demonstrate confidence by looking around when you walk instead of looking at the ground, or by smiling and making eye contact with those passing by.*

<u>Weak in Stature</u> – In our western society bigger is better and perceived as putting up more resistance. Being short, skinny, and or having less muscle mass than the average American citizen can make you a target if your stature is combined with a perceived lack of confidence.

A Note From EJ...You can strengthen your stature appearance through exercise, the clothes you wear, and the confidence that you exude as you participate in your daily activities.

<u>Shy</u> – Generally speaking, people who are naturally shy tend to not look strangers in the eyes as they pass. They often walk as if they don't want to be noticed and avoid situations where interaction with others could be possible. This makes it easy for attackers to swoop in close as shy individuals are not as aware of their immediate surroundings as others.

A Note From EJ...Shyness is another indicator of a lack of confidence from the predator's perception. Look around, pay attention to your surroundings, and engage others, if only with a smile or quick eye contact. Work to build confidence as predators seldom deal with confident people.

<u>Poor Posture</u> – How we carry ourselves says a lot about what we are willing to do should we encounter a compromising situation without ever having to say or physically demonstrate to others. Posture emulates our self-image. Slumping shoulders, shuffling feet, and hanging heads tell the criminal that we are easy prey.

A Note From EJ...I'm sure your mother or father at some time in your life said to you "Stand up straight." or "Hold your shoulders back." Poor posture is a neon sign to predators. Work on your posture. Standing straight demonstrates self-confidence.

Projecting Weakness - A trusting, gullible, but naïve attitude toward seemingly harmless strangers that causes a person to bare his or her soul to the person at the bar, next to you on the bus, or even in the grocery line, makes that person an easy target. In their naivety, these persons project their morals of goodness, friendliness, and belief that "since I wouldn't hurt you, you won't hurt me". Criminals love these people!

A Note From EJ...It is appropriate and even necessary to trust, be friendly, and engaging to those around you. Doing so, however, without first taking in your surroundings, being aware that the other person might actually harm you (date rape, for instance), and without thinking how much information about yourself you may be giving to someone who might want to hurt you is foolish. Don't be foolish. Look...Think...and then Act!

Here are a few key environmental situations that could subject you victimization:

Preoccupied with Something – when you are preoccupied with performing a task like loading groceries into your car or herding your children through a busy parking lot you are simply unaware of surroundings. This state of preoccupation allows criminals to advance on your position, placing them in a strategic location to dominate you. If your hands are full, you are not likely to defend yourself in time. If your headphones are on you are not likely to be aware of someone advancing on you. If you are deep in a heated conversation on the phone while standing outside your car, again, you are not likely to realize someone is sizing you up for an attack.

Nowhere To Run – Violent criminals look for targets of opportunity. As in the animal kingdom, predators like to ambush their prey. They look for environmental bottlenecks that physically trap their victims. For example, if you attend a baseball or football game and park in an unlighted field or yard several blocks away, getting to or getting into your car would provide the perfect opportunity for a car jacking. The same would be true if you park in a parking garage away from stairs or other means of immediate egress as your retreat is now futile.

Collateral Damage – Predators look for you to be in a situation that could prevent you from resisting their demands. A popular situation that predators look for is the threat of collateral damage. Collateral damage in this context implies that you have something to lose that is greater that the demands of the attacker. Should you put up resistance, for example, the predator may threaten that someone else may get hurt or killed. As a result, you allow the predator to take what he wants in order to prevent the threat from becoming a reality.

An example of this collateral damage approach is easily seen with a mother (or father) with small children.

When faced with a threat in such a situation, a mother's (or father's) immediate response is "whatever it takes to protect my kids". While considering the protection of the kids, however, you often forsake your own safety. Your reasoning is that if you comply with the predator the children will be unharmed. It is unlikely that your reasoning will prevail.

A Note From EJ...You cannot reason with or beg a predator – you must outmaneuver him

PREDATOR GOALS

A predator's goal is simple! To get what he wants. You have something he wants, so he sets about to get it. The "something" may be:

✓ Money

✓ Valuables

✓ Vehicle

✓ Weapons

✓ Drugs

✓ Control

✓ Sex

✓ Fear

...to name a few! You see, the goal is often the item, not the person. The person is in the way. Hurting or killing the person is, to the predator, merely a "necessary evil" required to accomplish the goal.

MENTAL STATE

"It's about selfishness ... the different manifestations of criminal behavior is just a matter of style."   Stanton Samenow, Ph.D.

While everyone, to some degree or another, is selfish, criminals, whether violent and angry or just angry, take selfishness to extremes. There are thousands upon thousands of books on crime, violence, criminology and criminal psychology. These books contain a lot of theories about the motivations of criminals. Let it be said that the theories purported by these books were developed by academia and medical personnel after interviewing and observing criminals from a position of influence over the criminals' immediate future (e.g. the psychologists were in a position to influence whether or not the criminal would be released or imprisoned). The relative positions of these professionals and researchers were controlled and therefore, safe.

As influencers of the criminal's future, the criminal recognizes the need to stay in the good graces of the interviewer. He attempts to do so often by trying to "get over" on the person. This is a normal dynamic in institutionalized settings where criminals are studied. It is also why I liken the attempt to understand the violent criminals in the institutional setting to that of studying bears in the zoo. While all kinds of important zoological information can be gathered when studying bears in a zoo, you still are not dealing with the beasts in their natural habitat. In a zoo setting, it is also unlikely that you will ever be on the receiving end of a bear's charge. Very few, if any, academic theorists have developed their theories about the nature of the criminal mind while looking down the business end of a gun held by a criminal.

In the last chapter I talked about intent or the "why" of the crime. It is in the act of determining intent that leads us to the decision for the appropriate course of action. In some cases, the mere criminal act alone is justification for us to return a violent, defensive response without having determined intent first. An example of this is a guy pulling a gun on you in the parking lot. At that point in time it doesn't matter what he wants. If you don't act to defend yourself you will probably die without ever knowing the "why" behind his actions and demands.

Take time to know local, state, and federal laws governing self-defense. Understanding the criteria that justifies self-defense is paramount to your confidence that you are acting within the law during the act. It also ensures that you will act appropriately after the act is completed. This means that you need a practical understanding of ways to stop the criminal rather than textbook knowledge on the how to "cure" him (talk him out of it) before he performs the act.

FORCE DECIDED

Unfortunately for you as the victim in this case, the attacker has predetermined what he is willing to do to obtain what he wants from you. Your disadvantage is that you don't know the extent of what that willingness is. Case in point, during the act of getting mugged, you comply with the predator's commands; yet, he shoots you anyway. From your perspective, you were doing what he wanted—you were complying—and you still got shot! Why? Because somewhere in that demented brain of his, he still saw you as a threat needing to be eliminated. I call it "*Comply and Die.*" You can <u>never</u> assume that through compliance you will be unharmed.

RESISTANCE

Predators have a sharp instinct. One way for an unarmed victim to survive such an attack is to "*get crazy*" on the attacker. Fight fire with fire by unleashing your "*animal within*". Fight back and do so with the utmost ferocity. Use the most brutal fighting options you have available, such as blinding him using your fingers to push his eyes into his head or crippling him with kicks or elbows. Then...escape! This may sound "*crazy*", but when you have no other option...it might be your best option!

Predators typically won't mess with you if they think you're crazier than they are.

TYPES OF VIOLENT ATTACKS

This list is not all-inclusive. I am including it to give you an understanding of what criminals want and how they might go about getting it. Remember what we have discussed earlier in this chapter and see if your demeanor, posture, and awareness could see it coming and more importantly...think about your level of "craziness".

See if you have enough craziness to be crazier than your predator. Do not become a victim.

Gang Initiation

- violent acts to obtain membership
- typically are random in nature
- use of multiple attackers

Drug Seekers

- unorthodox approaches
- no plan
- no limit on physical violence, though it usually escalates
- start slow, but gets angry quickly

Robbers

- typically uses intimidation first through a show of force
- speed is paramount
- planned to some degree
- set goal in mind
- often willing to kill

Car Jackers

- could be using it to get away from a previously committed crime
- urgency
- takes by surprise
- violent and angry

- speed is paramount
- you could be a hostage

Rapist

- mentally unstable
- needs to be in control
- you probably know him
- thinks you won't resist
- may use drugs to subdue victim
- victims can be murdered even after complying
- sodomized
- takes pleasure in your pain
- violent control during sex is often a turn-on

Home Invader

- planned to some degree
- knows you might be home
- might not stop at just physical assets
- collateral damage might make you compliant
- could be multiple assailants involved

A Note From EJ... Understanding your enemy gives you more information with which you can make a better decision.

Criminals do not die by the hands of the law.
They die by the hands of other men.

— George Bernard Shaw

SHEEP: people who depend on others to protect and take care of them.

SHEEPDOGS: those who are willing to face evil and defend themselves and the flock.

Which one are you? Find out here:

www.SheepdogSociety.org

CHAPTER 5

Heads Up

There are numerous burglaries and assaults that could have been prevented entirely. Unfortunately, most people tend subscribe to the notion that "crime won't happen to me." Regrettably, criminals thrive on unsuspecting, unprotected, and unprepared individuals. A complacent mindset is a criminal's number one turn-on.

Criminals are predators! They prey on those they perceive to be weak. It does not matter if you don't feel weak. If a criminal perceives you as weak, he will pounce! Let me be clear that when I refer to "weak," it has nothing to do with your physical or mental prowess; but everything to do with your lack of situational awareness and preparation.

SITUATIONAL AWARENESS

Situational awareness simply means being wholly, thoroughly aware of everything going on around you. This is true whether you are at home, at work, at the mall, at school, in a restaurant, driving, traveling, out for a walk or run, out with the guys or the girls ...well, you get the point—anywhere! You must know who is near you and what is going on all around at all times. Primarily, the criminal seeks out individuals who appear to be in "la la land" and unaware that they are a few feet away from a probable attack.

SITUATIONAL PREPARATION

Situational preparedness results from understanding what vulnerabilities you, your family and your home possess that a potential criminal could exploit. You should consider having a professional conduct a comprehensive *Threat Assessment* of your personal and residential security. [Email me if you need help identifying a reputable professional in your area.] This assessment is key to identifying the security flaws in your everyday life. Flaws increase your susceptibility to becoming the victim of criminal activity.

It is not enough to lock your doors at night. It is not enough to own a German Shepherd, Doberman, or any other "large and scary" four-legged creature. It is not enough to just carry pepper spray or Mace. You must know *who* the criminal is likely to target for their next crime. You must know *what* the criminal is looking for in a potential victim. You must know *where* the criminal is likely to conduct his next attack. You must know *when* the criminal is likely to strike. And, finally, you must have some understanding as to *why* the criminal is committing this violent act. Remember criminals are predators and they attack those they perceive to be weak.

A Note From EJ...Take a look from the outside in. Could a criminal perceive you as weak? Weak = "unaware", "unprepared", "complacent", "unbelieving"

Many politicians, law officers and criminal researchers feel that crime is a pandemic that is quickly overtaking the societies of the world. With economies in recession around the world, fraud, corruption, theft, and violent crime is rampant. In realizing that hurt people hurt others, you should understand that the chance of your or someone you love becoming a victim of crime is no long shot. It is a possibility—likely, a reality. Use the advice in this book to close up loopholes in your private life that may enable potential criminals the opportunity to penetrate.

Remember, a fort with weak cornerstones will quickly fall and a castle built on sand will come crumbling down in a short time. Naivety for you should be a thing of the past. Even after you apply what you learn from this book, continue to acquire skills in self-protection, strategic living and seek wisdom above all else. It is not the intent of this chapter to raise your fear level, but to rather serve as a practical preventative survival methodology.

SURVIVAL METHODOLOGY

KEEP A PROPER VIEW ON LIFE

As we go about our daily lives, you and I are constantly evaluating and re-evaluating. Sometimes we elevate one thing over another. Sadly, the thing we just elevated was of no real importance, but we just made that unimportant thing the most important thing in our lives. The unimportant thing at that moment could be money, a relationship, an asset, a job or a person, yet we elevated it by our own choice.

Conduct a priority check on a regular basis to ensure you have life in perspective and that nothing that you value has become out of sync in relation to the rest of life. Failure to do this could place you at a risk of becoming a victim of crime. Potential criminals often study their victims. They see those areas where the victim is highly invested emotionally as a possible penetration point.

PROTECT YOURSELF

The benefit of vulnerability is that it reminds you and those around you that you are human. In our current society, vulnerability should be run through a sounding board of wisdom before being expressed. The reasons for this suggestion ties in with the point mentioned above.

WATCH THE COMPANY YOU KEEP

It has been said, "Bad company corrupts good character." This is true. People also judge us on the company we keep. Often however, the seemingly most innocent person can turn out to be the most vicious at heart when provoked. This is, therefore, not a foolproof methodology. I can tell you from experience, however, that keeping a small circle of close friends whose actions and lifestyle you have observed in a variety of circumstances is wise. Exposing yourself to a large community of people on a regular basis without observing their actions and reactions is foolish. The best example of this is the bar scene. The bar scene is ripe for pickpockets, rape drugs, Good judgment on personal safety requires that you limit your availability to crowds of people that you don't know or know about.

KEEP STRANGERS OUT OF YOUR HOME

Due to the economy "living with a buddy" is becoming a more common trend. Bachelor apartments are now housing several "buddies" because of the shared expenses and the relatively cheaper living costs while sacrificing space. Families are even fast reducing their living space. The reason for mentioning this is that you or your "buddies" can easily invite a vicious criminal into your home or onto your property without being aware of it. Don't pick up strangers and invite them into your home. Don't easily go home with strangers either.

HOME SECURITY

This depends on the area in which you live. Some areas are more prone to crime than others. Therefore, consider the level of home security needed within this perspective. Comply with the minimum security requirements of your insurance company.

Insurance companies share claims data. This means that your insurance company has a large database of information available to them. Your agent can narrow the information to your particular community and offer security suggestions based on relevant and recent loss history for the area in which you reside.

Although not foolproof, I highly recommend that you take precautionary security measures. Strive to have a little more security installed than your neighbors do. Having just a little additional security may make your neighbors' houses more attractive to an opportunist thief or armed robber at crunch time.

LIMIT DANGEROUS OBJECTS IN YOUR HOME

Because a vicious murder can be committed with an item like a garden spade, one should be careful and responsible when it comes to your living environment. Keep dangerous objects, like firearms, safely locked away according to the laws of your state when not in use.

DON'T LEAVE YOUR VALUABLES OUT

Keep valuables like expensive jewelry, cash, and passports under lock and key when not in use. Even putting costume jewelry and antique chachkis (trinkets) in a drawer keeps the "peeping" criminal from eyeing things that he might want to see up close while you are out.

BE SKEPTICAL OF YOUR HOME-ASSISTANTS

Some families have maids, home care assistants for the ill or elderly, gardeners, in-home childcare providers and perhaps music teachers that come and go from the house. Use a reputable agency to locate such assistants. If you hire directly, take the time and make the small investment necessary to check credentials and references. Many thefts and armed robberies, once investigated, point straight to the home assistant.

NEIGHBOR-HOOD WATCH

Some communities have neighborhood watches or resort to protecting their communities by gating off certain residential streets and appointing a guard to man an entrance point for these areas. All these things are not foolproof, but serve as deterrents. Thieves would, more often than not, rather bother the suburb next door that doesn't have these little inconveniences.

DON'T WALK ALONE AT NIGHT OR IN POTENTIALLY UNSAFE AREAS

In some communities, this is still safe, but in most, this is viewed as a high risk and caution should be exercised. There is an element of safety in numbers and to deny this is foolishness.

BREAK ROUTINE AS MUCH AS POSSIBLE

Suspecting criminals watch for a routine in a potential victim's lifestyle. The more information they have about the victim, the better. Try to not arrive at home or leave for work at exactly the same time every day. Control freaks who live by strict agendas, time frames and strict routines are at risk of being victims of crime. Being overly controlling of your environment is not going to protect you from this possible risk. Everything in balance is the key.

BUILD A REPUTATION OF INTEGRITY

Ensure you keep your life clean and pure at all times. Live above reproach. This way, nobody will be able to blackmail you, be successful in bribing you to protect information or correctly point fingers of blame at you. Guard your heart and your reputation. Teach your children to do the same. Your family deserves this.

BE AWARE OF OPPORTUNITIES FOR THOSE *SNATCH-&-GRAB* ACTS

The basics you've heard since the teen years still apply now and should be taught to your teens:

- Hold on tightly to your handbag or briefcase in public places.
- Look for potential pickpockets and check your pockets often.
- Do not flash cash in public.
- Do not leave your cell phone or purse on the car seat next to you while driving, especially in stop-and-go traffic.
- Keep your car doors locked when inside the car.
- Ensure passenger doors are locked when getting gas.
- Always lock your car.

A Note From EJ...While you can't possibly prevent all crime from happening, you can reduce your exposure. Criminals search for possible victims. I don't want to discount random crime from the equation but in reality you can't predict nor plan for "random". Being at the right place at the wrong time might happen. When it does though, you have to make some very serious and potentially life-altering decisions. Awareness is key. Being aware of your situation and mentally prepared for a fight gives you the highest chance for survival.

The successful warrior is the average man with laser-like focus.

-Bruce Lee

There are only three types of people...

Wolves. Sheep. Sheepdogs.

Which one are you? Find out here:

www.SheepdogSociety.org

CHAPTER 6

Mindset

To establish the ideal mindset for thwarting a violent criminal you must first understand how we compute information under stress. One of the best ideologies used today is the *O.O.D.A. Loop* (OODA Loop) created by Colonel John Boyd. This loop of intellectual computation reveals some interesting systematic responses we naturally endure in order to come to the "action" phase of our response.

If we understand how our minds compute provided or perceived information and we learn the nuances of each of the four steps in the OODA Loop, we can train ourselves to move quickly through the steps to the "A" or *action* step. When dealing with a violent criminal hell-bent on doing you harm, you have only a very few seconds to make a decision. Training ourselves to make decisions quickly allows us to reduce decision time thus getting into the fight or away from the fight sooner. Time is life! The more time we take to act against the criminal, the more disadvantaged we are.

OODA LOOP

US Air Force Colonel John Boyd (1927-1997) was arguably one of the most important American military thinkers in the 20th century. Colonel Boyd is best remembered for his formulation of the *OODA Loop,* also known as the "OODA Cycle" or "Boyd's Loop". The OODA Loop is a model of the competitive decision-making by individuals and groups alike. Understanding the OODA Loop allows you to prepare general tactics for commonly encountered situations and specific tactics when detailed circumstances are known ahead of time.

Colonel Boyd left his mark on air combat tactics, maneuver warfare, and what we now call "fourth-generation warfare." Although all branches of the military felt his influence, the U.S. Marine Corps felt his influence the most. General Charles Krulak, former Marine commander wrote, *"From John Boyd we learned about competitive decision-making on the battlefield – compressing time, using time as an ally."*

Boyd's personality was very aggressive. Not unexpectedly, he favored the offense as exemplified by the blitzkrieg or "lightning war" advocated by the Chinese master Sun-Tzu, and the British partisan leader T. E. Lawrence, better known as Lawrence of Arabia. Boyd's OODA Loop reflects the influence of these two great strategists.

The OODA Loop shows that you first have to get information (Observe). Once you have the information, you now determine what it means to you and what can you do about it (Orient).

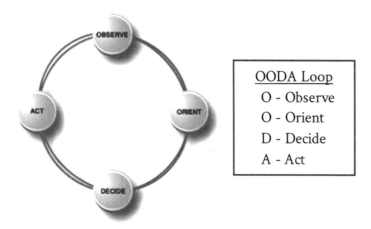

OODA Loop
O - Observe
O - Orient
D - Decide
A - Act

With information and the application of that information to your current situation, you can make a decision (Decide) and take appropriate action (Act). On the flip side, your understanding of the OODA Loop can allow you to surmise quickly what your opponent is thinking and affect his thinking by affecting the information he receives. With quick action on your part, you may also change his orientation of the information you affected to your advantage.

Robert Greene, author of *The 48 Laws of Power,* wrote his international blockbuster book as a practical guide for anyone who wants power or wants to arm himself against power. In a blog article called "OODA and You," Greene stresses that the proper mindset for gaining power is "to let go a little, to allow some of the chaos to become part of [your] mental system, and to use it to [your] advantage by simply creating more chaos and confusion for the opponent".

Using Greene's approach, you funnel the inevitable chaos of the assault back in the direction of the attacker. An entity (whether an individual or an organization) that can process this cycle quickly—observing and reacting to unfolding events more rapidly than an opponent—can "get inside" the opponent's decision cycle and gain the advantage. The more adept you are with the thought process of the cycle, the more likely you are to be able to feed "bad" information to your opponent, often confusing him and possibly getting the upper hand in the battle more quickly than expected.

CONCEPT

Processing through the OODA Loop requires that you observe the situation, orient yourself within the observed situation determining actions and reactions, decide what to do by choosing an action, and then, doing the action. The process then repeats itself. It is possible to go through the OODA Loop several times in a single minute.

- ➤ Observe means to know what is happening through any of your five senses, not just sight.

- ➤ Orient means to understand the meaning of what you observed as it relates to actions and reactions.

- ➤ Decide is weighing the options available and picking one.

- ➤ Act is carrying out the decision.

REACTIONARY GAP

Simply put, the *reactionary gap* is the distance between two individuals in which an action can be rendered. Here is an example. If two people are standing a foot apart facing each other, the first one is instructed to touch the second one as fast as he can while the second one is told to slap away the first person's hand before he gets touched. The second person will never succeed because he has to go through the full OODA loop before he can react. By that time the first person will have already touched him.

As the distance between the two persons increases and the instructions are repeated, the second person becomes more likely to have enough time to react because the greater distance gives him enough time to observe and orient himself to the threat. The greater distance also adds time to decide which hand to slap down and to take that action because it takes longer for the hand of the first person to touch. Because the second person already knows what the first person is going to do and has made a decision on how he will react, the second person now moves almost instantly from observe to act.

APPLICATION FOR GROUND FIGHTING

Your opponent's OODA loop can be broken in a ground fight by simply changing tactics before he can get to the act portion of the loop. If I have an opponent in a joint lock or choke hold and he starts to make headway against my hold, I would quickly switch tactics and attack another limb. He would react by starting his OODA Loop all over again to find a way to break this new hold. Before he could make much headway in his OODA Loop, I would switch again and get him in a different hold. The entire time we are fighting, he is expending much more energy that I am, getting tired sooner physically as well as mentally. That is because I am always ahead of him in the OODA Loop switching tactics before he can respond effectively. Throughout the fight I am using little effort and great technique. My opponent is getting fatigued fighting against my attacks. His fatigue gives me complete control of my OODA Loop and my control of his OODA Loop even stronger.

APPLICATION FOR SWAT TEAM ENTRIES

The SWAT team makes entry on a room by throwing a flashbang. A flashbang is a non-lethal explosive device used to temporarily disorient an enemy's senses. It produces a blinding flash of light and loud noise without causing permanent injury. While the suspect and his victims are disoriented by the light and concussion, the team enters and engages the suspect before he can react.

The flashbang breaks the *orient* phase of the suspect's OODA Loop. Until the suspect can regain his sight and a slight sense of hearing, he cannot move on to the *decide* and *act* phases, thus rendering him incapacitated.

APPLICATION FOR YOU

In each of these examples, action beats reaction. Yet often we have to react to circumstances and people around us. The trick is to use our knowledge of the OODA Loop to take the offense away from our opponent. Generally that means overtaking him in the

OODA Loop by being faster or by slowing him down. All of this should occur in a fraction of a second.

We will repeat this thought process with every action that we take using information about our opponent's reactions to what we are doing. In most deadly encounters, we are already behind in the OODA Loop when the fight starts. The bad guy has already gone through his OODA Loop and is acting while you are observing. In order to regain the advantage, we must move through the OODA Loop quickly processing the threat and act accordingly. There is no time to second guess our decision to act. Acting quickly forces our opponent back to the *observe* phase. To illustrate, consider the following scenario:

You are filling your vehicle with gas. The occupant of the vehicle at the next pump suddenly opens his door and gets out with a gun in his hand. Bad Guy = Act; You = Observe. At this initial phase of the battle, the  bad guy has the advantage. He has already gone through his OODA Loop and is about to shoot you dead. You, on the other hand, are caught flat-footed. You are filling your vehicle with a flammable liquid (gas) probably in an area where you have no cover. How do you regain the advantage? You quickly sidestep as you draw your weapon. Sidestepping means that you are no longer standing where the suspect thought you would be. Now, You = Act; Bad Guy =Observe.

Just a simple movement like sidestepping can make the bad guy go through his OODA Loop again while you are laying accurate fire on him. In a gunfight, a quick shift in OODA Loop processing often determines who lives and who dies. This scenario is simple, but realistic—and it does show how the OODA Loop works. While your mind will need to go through the entire loop with each new piece of information presented, the bottom line is this:

The faster you can go from "Observe" to "Act" the more advantage you will have.

Making the transitions required between *observe* and *act* quickly requires training. There are many ways to train your body and mind. Sparring, force-on-force training and scenario training are examples of excellent training approaches for OODA Loop transitions.

When participating in formal training is not possible, another way to train is to visualize various scenarios that may occur in your particular environments—in your home, your office building, your office, your car, your boat, on your bike. As you visualize a particular environment, develop a course of action. Ask yourself, "What will I do if a predator and I meet in (name the place)?" Visualize a situation. See yourself walk into your office only to meet a predator. Orient yourself in that situation noting egress areas, distances, lighting, furniture, and other parts of the surroundings. Decide how you will react by asking yourself, "If he does this, I will do _____.". This is an effective technique for training your thinking to move quickly through your OODA Loop. When you perform multiple visualizations, you become oriented and decided. You are able to move directly from *observe* to *act*. You also increase your confidence to handle such threatening situations.

Visualization training is a favorite among athletes and has proven very beneficial. Many weight loss programs suggest visualizing yourself at your chosen weight. Years ago, "dress for success" was a popular preparation approach recommended by recruiters that started with visualizing yourself in the job you wanted to get.

Of utmost importance in visualization training is your ability to maintain situational awareness. If you are not aware of your surroundings, you will not properly assess the threat. A poor or incorrect assessment of a threat is doomed to fail. This brings us to the *Cooper's Color Code of Awareness*.

COOPER'S COLOR CODE

OF AWARENESS

Colonel Jeff Cooper (1920-2008), another U.S. Marine Corps veteran, developed *Cooper's Color Code of Awareness*. Colonel Cooper was one of the most prolific firearms trainers and theorists of the modern age. He founded the American Pistol Institute in 1976. During his lifetime, Colonel Cooper authored many books and articles relating to gunfighting.

Through the years, various trainers and schools have modified *Cooper's Color Code of Awareness*. The Federal government uses a modification of Cooper's color code as a scale to indicate, "force protection" or threat levels. You might have noticed a colored threat indicator on the door to a government building. If so, you have met *Cooper's Color Code of Awareness* already. To keep things simple and to encourage further reading on the scale, I will focus on Colonel Cooper's original scale shown here (white, yellow, orange, red).

| Unaware and Unprepared | Relaxed but Alert | Specific Alert | Fight Trigger |

The *Color Code of Awareness* has nothing to do with tactical situations. It does not represent physical alertness levels. Instead, it indicates the state of mind in which you should function relative to possible or potential threats. Cooper identified levels of mental attention and associated each level with a particular color. White indicates the lowest level of alertness; red indicates the highest level of alertness. As the color intensity increases so should our level of alertness increase.

Unaware and Unprepared

"Oh, my God! Is this really happening?"
In this mental state you are totally relaxed, not paying attention to your surroundings. Should a threat come along, you are not pre-

pared to defend yourself against it and will likely be asking yourself if the threat is even real.

Relaxed but Alert

"I might have to defend myself today."
In this mental state, you are relaxed, but alert in your surroundings for possible threats. This is the condition you should be in throughout your day.

Specific Alert

"I might have to shoot someone sooner than later." In this mental state, you have identified a potential threat. You are focused on the threat with your mental trigger set. "If that person does X, I will need to stop them." Your weapon usually remains holstered. If the threat proves to be nothing, you return to the yellow mental state.

Fight Trigger

"If X happens, I will shoot that person." X happens and the fight is on!
This mental state indicates that your "fight trigger" has activated. You are actually in the fight.

A Note From EJ...Applying the Color Code of Awareness should become a daily occurrence for you. Think about it throughout the day and evaluate what condition you find yourself in. Condition Yellow is where you should be most of the time. If you drift into condition White, you are putting yourself at risk. When you catch yourself there, wake up and get back to Yellow. Study the OODA Loop and Color Code of Awareness. Incorporate them into your daily activities. When the moment of truth comes and you decisively win your deadly encounter, you'll be glad you did!

I must study politics and war that my sons may have liberty to study mathematics and philosophy.

-John Adams

"Warriors Aren't Born. They're Made."

We Offer Real-World, Live Training Events.
For Info Go To:

www.ModernWarrior.org

CHAPTER 7

Science of Gunfighting

G unfight! The fictional version of what our mind's eye quickly conjures up when we hear the word "gunfight" comes from what movies and television would like us to believe—that a gunfight is simply two Old West gunfighters squaring off with each other on a dusty street. This over-romanticized image of the gunfight was born in the dime novels of the late 19th century and perpetuated in silent film era.

In actuality, the *real* gunfights of the Old West were rarely that civilized. In fact, several inaccuracies are consistently included in these romanticized gunfights. One inaccuracy is that actual planning for a gunfight to happen was very rare. Gunfights usually started in the heat of the moment when tempers flared, aided more often than not with a little "dark bottle" courage.

Another inaccuracy captured on film repeatedly is one party calling out their enemy for dueling action in the street. Instead, most gunfights took place wherever the fight started. They also didn't occur at a distance of

15 paces, with each gunfighter taking one shot, one falling dead to the ground, and the other standing as a hero before a dozen gathered onlookers. Instead, these fights were usually close-up and personal with repeated shots blasted from "six shooters." Innocent bystanders hit by stray bullets were not uncommon. After the shooting stopped it was often difficult to tell who even won until

the black power smoke had cleared. It is important to note that the gunfights today, just as back in the Old West, are rarely planned.

Today's modern gunfight in a combat zone either results from an ambush or a raid. The ambush is the more common of the two. An ambush causes soldiers to react by devising a counter-ambush plan and then implementing it. Luckily for our soldiers they left the FOB (forward operating base) following the #1 and #2 rules for gunfighting:

Rule #1 - Bring A Gun.

Rule #2 - Bring Friends With Guns!

Historians and enthusiasts continue to study the guns and gunfights of the past as well as today's gunfighting techniques and approaches. Many gunfighters like our soldiers and those who want to use a gun effectively if the situation demands it commit to perfect their gunfighting skills and tactics. More importantly, they commit their mindset in much the same way as a Samurai Warrior committed his mindset, allowing that mindset to take over his body's actions and reactions. All too often we as 2nd Amendment expressing gun carriers prepare for our deadly encounter on a static range with a goal of punch-

ing as small a hole as possible into a paper target. Doing so indicates that our mindset is this: We will knowingly square off to a front-facing threat and victoriously defeat him with our superior shooting skills. Then, we will turn to the beautiful woman we just saved, give her a head nod, and say "Are you alright?"

We are often guilty of consistently training on those aspects of shooting we are naturally good at accomplishing. The strong-handed weaver or the isosceles stance is the common picture of the guy next to you, and more than likely, you too! While that is a good start for the beginner, the true warrior has to be ready for the yet-unknown fight lurking in the future.

To prepare for that unknown fight with the unknown fighter in an unknown location under unknown circumstances, you must break out of your comfort zone and train those things at which you do not already excel. You must train your mind to see things that you do not see now because you are not looking for them. You must perceive the fighting space, move in it ruthlessly, and dominate the fight.

To understand the dynamics of a gunfight you need to expand your education beyond just stance and trigger pulling. When thinking about countering violence through a gunfight or handling threats of any kind, there are four factors I want you to consider. I want you to integrate these four factors into your thinking so that when you are studying, while you are training, and simply when you are out and about, the principles of these four factors are second nature to you. Once you understand the *Science of Gunfighting*, your training, and ultimately your fighting, will take on a whole new meaning.

THREAT VECTOR

The first factor to consider is the *threat vector*. The threat vector is the line of approach the threat (the perpetrator or intruder) is taking directly toward you. Whether the threat will be a physical attack with someone's hands or a knife, or if the threat will be a bullet, the path that is the most direct line between it and you is the threat vector. The threat could come from any direction, not just the one or two scenarios you have played over and over in your head. For example, you may have the scenario of the threat coming through your bedroom door or from your closet. What if it comes from the bathroom or from behind the drapes on the window? Plan, anticipate, prepare. The threat vector sets up the reaction and action requirements and helps define the next three factors.

SPACE

The second factor to consider is *space*. Space is the immediate area in which you must deal with the threat. To help define the space start by asking yourself these questions,

What is around me?

Where can I go?"

Where can he go?

How close am I to the threat?

Is there anything in the space that I can use to tilt the advantage in my favor?

Use these questions to establish where you are so you can figure out how not to be there for the punch to land, the knife to cut, or the bullet to hit.

TIME

The third factor is that of *time*. Particularly in a gunfight, the threat vector always dictates time. Space may or may not impacted the factor of time.

Just know this...time is <u>not</u> dictated nor is it impacted by your physical ability to draw or move off line of attack.

When thinking about time, ask yourself...

Do I have time to run away?

Can I get to my weapon in time to defend myself?

Do I have time to secure my kids or do I have to act now?

How much time will it take for me to improve my cover?

In your scenario practice, did you successfully recognize the threat, process it, control your reaction and take the proper action before the intruder closed the distance on the threat vector and took you down? I hope so! It's a worthy goal to works towards.

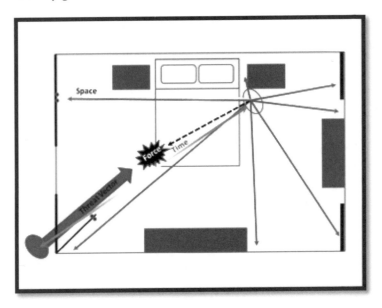

FORCE

The last factor is *force*. Force is the immediate threat brought to bear by the attacker. In a physical attack, such as a hand-to-hand fight, using your opponent's force against him is always superior to overpowering him.

There are issues to trying to overpower someone, however. It is possible that in your effort to overpower your opponent, you could apply too much power causing unnecessary injury to him, landing yourself in costly (and perhaps embarrassing) legal trouble. In court the idea of "appropriate force" to neutralize the threat applies. In the eyes of the court, your counterattack should be equal to—not greater than—the force brought on you. Remember, the bad guy picks the time, selects the place, and determines the amount of force that will be involved, much like in an ambush situation our troops often face.

Our "scenarios" are just that, thoughts of possible situations that could have no bearing on the reality of the current situation. That's why we train for everything, even as silly as it sounds, you never know when or where your encounter will happen.

As with hand-to-hand fighting using your own body weight against an attacker grants you more options and requires less motion and body strength when dealing with them. Nearly always, this advantage keeps you in the fight longer because your fatigue sets in slower. As it relates to gunfighting, it's not who fires first, but who fires and hits first! Accurate hits end gunfights fast!

SCIENCE

So how do these four factors interact with each other to make science?

Science comes from the Latin word *scientia* meaning knowledge. Its common definition is "knowledge attained through study or practice and covering general truths of the operation of general laws." Science offers a systematic approach to acquiring knowledge. Its purpose is to produce useful models of reality through the knowledge it provides. The knowledge provided by science is the type that can be rationally explained and reliably applied.

Over the course of the 19th century, the word "science" was increasingly associated with the scientific method. The scientific method became accepted as a disciplined way to study the natural world, including physics, chemistry, geology and biology.

Science, through observation and experiments, helps define principles and express theories. From these principles and theories, knowledge forms. To ensure that we obtain all possible knowledge, we must identify and understand our personal learning style and then the learning styles of those we are most often around.

LEARNING STYLES

The three most common types in no particular order include:

> *Spatial:* You prefer to learn through pictures and images such as videos, demonstrations, and comic strips; the sense of seeing set in a context

> *Linguistic:* You prefer to learn through words, whether spoken or written, allowing your mind to set the context; the senses of seeing and hearing

> *Kinesthetic:* You prefer to learn as you use your body to move and your hands to do; the sense of touch

The majority of us learn proficiently by doing and through movement rather than reading, hearing lecture, or viewing images. The kinesthetic learning style refers to acquiring knowledge through movement. It is the movement that allows our senses to gain the most information about the environment we are in at the time.

If you found your learning style to be spatial, watch some of my videos on YouTube and check out others on the Legally Concealed website. Take classes that put you in situations and practice in your various environments. Try going to your church or synagogue on your lunch break or at night when some other meeting is going on and practice in the hallways, restrooms, stairwells and corners. Find times that you can visit and visualize incidents in other places that you frequent. Check out other videos on the Internet. Practice your color code awareness skill and check your OODA Loop progress often.

If you found your learning style to be linguistic then this book is right up your alley! Read, attend lectures, take classes. Practice your color code awareness skill wherever you go and check your OODA Loop progress often. Visualize—it's like reading your own mind! Pretty cool, huh?

Incorporating the use of movement in your training will reinforce the four factors just discussed. Most gunfighting classes will teach you, upon recognition of a threat, to MOVE! To move means to get off the threat vector and gain space. Recognizing and practicing

the four factors will ensure that you can and will naturally enact them when under stress. As a kinesthetic learn-
er, you instantly recognize the factors, but without the
knowledge to utilize this information, we rarely make
the right decisions.

RETENTION VS. COMPREHENSION

This brings us to another aspect of learning: retention versus comprehension. Retention is much like
cramming the night before a test. We soak up as much
information as we can to accurately regurgitate the next
day then forget it a day or week later when we don't use
it again. If we do use the information again quickly, then
we retain the information longer. Reusing the information often is key for long-term retention.

Comprehension goes beyond retention in that it
is the application of the information and therefore, reus-
able regardless of the context or situation. Understanding that the majority of us are kinesthetic learners,
getting out of our chairs and doing will lead to comprehension. Let me illustrate. Telling you to recognize that
a threat is behind you, pivot on your weak side front foot
to the rear and draw will only trigger what you are capable of mentally picturing and playing out in your mind.
The act is not committed to memory. Because it is not
set in your memory, it is not able to be applied correctly
in a "time is life" situation when you are under stress or
constrained by threat or coercion, which describes *duress*.

Conversely, if I demonstrate the series of movements to you and have you do the series over and over

again through several shooting classes, the movements associated with the act become instinct, reactionary, and automatic. They surpass regurgitation or retention and become useful to you in a context other than my shooting classes. This indicates that you now comprehend the act you learned through movement.

At this level of learning, comprehension, you will have the knowledge and skill to perform the series correctly and upon demand. This is because you used your preferred learning style or modality to seal it into your mind at the useful level called "comprehension." It also explains why attending only one or two shooting classes may not prepare you for a gunfight despite what some instructors will tell you.

As you get a chance, ask other family members or work colleagues how they prefer to learn. Use their learning style the next time you want to get some information to stick. Let me know what happens. Email me! I will respond.

Ok! Bear with me. A little "professor-speak" goes a long way toward improving your gunfighting and your ability to work with others in stressful situations. This is good stuff!

BLOOM'S TAXONMY OF LEARNING

In the 1950's, a committee of premier educators led by Benjamin Bloom identified six levels within the learning process. These six levels are now known as "Bloom's Taxonomy of Learning Domains" or just "Bloom's Taxonomy." The internet is full of information on the taxonomy if you wish to learn more than I will share here. The diagram you see provides the six levels and offers some explanation about each level. Take a minute now to read through the diagram from the bottom up before I continue.

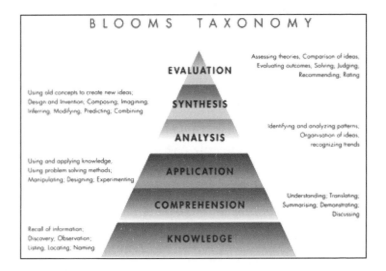

The levels go from simplest (Knowledge) to most involved (Evaluation). As we identified learning styles and applied them, and came to understand the difference between retention and comprehension, we moved through the first two of the six levels: knowledge and comprehension. Application is the level at which we use the knowledge we gained and retained. Let's talk about application and threats.

APPLICATION

   In any situation, recognition of the threat and its vector happens first. With it, your mind has established the type of threat. As stated earlier, you will never know from which direction the threat will appear until it is ready to be discovered. This puts us on the defensive. Working defensively against a threat is like playing defense on a football team. They act and we react. Our reaction requires that we recall knowledge, determine if it could apply to this situation and then, if that knowledge that could apply would, in fact, improve this situation. If so, we apply it—Bloom's third level.

When we train, say for instance with our back to the threat, we are preparing our instincts (automatic movements) to use the knowledge we gained through kinesthetic learning to perform properly and accordingly. This improved performance gives us the advantage of managing our space and time better.

Once the threat and its vector are known we must compute the relative space in which we have to operate. Space encompasses not only distance between you and the threat, but also your area of movement away from the threat. If we are in our home and a window was just broken, we must determine quickly how to react. This act of determining is eating up precious time so understanding space is critical.

If you have watched the spy movies like the Jason Bourne types, you will often see our hero entering into a restaurant or other type of establishment and noting the entrances, exits, and types of obstacles. Well, our OGA (other government agencies) operatives really do this during real world missions. They determine their "space" while playing mental gymnastics on possible avenues of attack, cover and exit. They go in anticipating a fight and preparing for victory. They count themselves lucky when a gunfight doesn't happen.

We can do this in our own home! We can look at how our bedroom or safe room is laid out noting our possible movement options. We can look at how we can manipulate this space to tilt the fight to our advantage. Is there a chest of drawers we can throw down in front of our door thus slowing his entrance into the room? Is there a window we can use to escape? There are many other considerations that you can question relative to your own environment, but you get the idea.

Most times when you hear of a home invasion, the victim has cowered in a closet hoping the predator will not discover their hiding spot. Maybe that was the victim's only option. If we understand our space, we won't need to cower because we will know our options and give ourselves a greater chance to fight and win.

Time is key! Time for us means that we can, in fact, devise a plan. However, we didn't set the time for this event. He did. Now, we must manage it ruthlessly.

Based on our threat recognition and its vector and our knowledge of our space, we can decide what we have time to do in our given space. When we train we occasionally use shot timers to help us gauge our overall speed and proficiency on a particular drill. We can use tools like a shot timer to elevate stress just as can use them to push us to perform at a level higher than we thought possible. Well, certainly there won't be a physical shot timer in your space during an invasion, but effectively hitting your threat before he hits you is winning in any book.  Working under stress, like with a timer, prepares our instincts and reflexes to function properly without conscious guidance from our brains. It will certainly improve our ability to hit the target our barrel is grinning at.

Let me impress this upon you: If you have the time, opportunity and capacity to leave, then do it.

If not, get to doing what it is you're going to do!

At this point, you should be confident that you can now determine the force you need to apply within the vector, time, and space you estimate in order to deter, deflect, or defeat the threat. Remember, in a gun-fight, the first rule is *Bring A Gun!* If you left it in your car or resting comfortably in the safe, your gun does you no good. Bring your gun!

As a situation unfolds and you need to skin that smoke wagon of yours out of its holster, you will un-doubtedly want to apply the four concepts we discussed: threat vector, space, time, and force. All of your training (or lack thereof) will culminate in a blink on an eye. Many people involved in a gunfight say that time slowed down making everything seem surreal. That is because our minds are processing the events at a rate higher than we can react. Training under stress increases our poten-tial for correct actions within the appropriate timetable with favorable results.

The *science of gunfighting* occurs when the four concepts—threat vector, space, time and force—come together with the physical actions of your body. Your mind will only tell your body to do what you have trained it to do...every other action is wrapped in panic!

Hopefully, you now have a better understanding of why our military is so successful when engaging our enemies abroad. The military uses these concepts start-ing on day one of entry and continues to delve deeper in the science of gunfighting in order to bring perfection to the battlefield. Perfection after a military gunfight is the attacker dying for his cause and the soldier eating break-fast the next morning. For you, perfection is staying alive and uninjured while ensuring, to the best of your ability, that those around you do the same.

Science enables us to define appropriate and proper actions and reactions. Knowledge aids us as we define those actions and reactions at both the conscious and subconscious levels, thus converting instinct into action.

Animals use instinct. They don't know or understand why they do particular actions; they just do them. Not always is their "doing" the right thing or the best thing for them. We as humans have a deep intellectual understanding of ourselves and our environment. We can and should use this knowledge to make the best decisions. Injecting the four concepts of the *science of gunfighting* into our training gives us many advantages in a gunfight, but only if we train often and with a purpose. Although science may seem complicated, this is not...

The best way not get punched, slashed, or shot is simple:

DON'T BE THERE!

Don't be there...move off the vector!

Don't be there...gain or take away space before your attacker does!

Don't be there...recognize time and respond accordingly!

And if you are there...apply force appropriately

In preparing for battle I have always found that plans are useless, but planning is indispensable.

- General Dwight D. Eisenhower

Are You A Sheep Or Sheepdog?
Find out here:
www.SheepdogSociety.org

CHAPTER 8

The Fight

The scariest time in your life will come should you have to defend your existence on this planet in a violent encounter. Your adrenaline will spike to a level you have never experienced before. Your eyes will widen to the point of breaking the connective tissue holding them into your eye sockets and your nostrils will not be able to flare enough to suck the amount of oxygen your lungs will be demanding. Your stomach will close off and you might even lose control of your bowels. Lactic acid will build rapidly in your muscles, tightening your every move while your feet will feel as if you are wearing concrete boots. All of these will happen almost simultaneously to your physical body at the same time your mind will be processing information and devising a plan for survival. There will be a mix of autonomic nervous systems reactions fighting with conscious panic.

It just got real!

The short the situation is-this: Figure it out quickly and get moving! You will have to rely on your current physical stamina, past experiences, training, and a small amount of luck to survive. Everything that you are capable of doing has just culminated in this one event. You now have to execute your actions timely and accurately. I can't stress enough that this will happen fast! Actually...faster than fast! It will be on you in mere seconds. You will have even less time to act.

Until now you might have had some training, oh, awhile back and maybe even war-gamed a similar scenario a few times in your head. Of course, those scenarios all ended with you being victorious. Well, this is reality and I'm quite sure that in your war gaming, there wasn't this rush of physical and mental responses clouding your decisions and hindering your movements. As you go through the OODA Loop process, you are hit like a MAC truck with information and physical responses that are all competing for your decisions.

In a real life confrontation, you will not rise to the occasion; you will default to the highest level of training you have mastered! Let me say that again—the highest level *mastered*. Everything else you will do will be done out of panic. When in a state of panic, you have no conscious control over your actions. You are in stimulus overload. Your body will revert to its natural reaction of *fight or flight*. In flight mode, hopefully, you will realize that you are trying to move *away* from the threat. Under the fight response you might charge *towards* the threat without a plan for victory. Both actions can get you killed. Without trained intuitive responses, you are left with the "luck factor". Luck, sadly, doesn't choose a side in a fight.

In most deadly encounters, one side gains the advantage of surprise. This allows the advantaged side to compel the other side into compliance through the perceived disparity of their situation. This disparity comes from the situation failing to present a clear way out thus making it futile to resist. He has won! You are left with no choice (because this is how you perceive the situation) but to comply...and die.

There is no worse feeling then that of forced disparity. It is the feeling of complete brokenness. I liken it to the African water buffalo attacked by a pack of hungry lions. They have him by the neck. The water buffalo is not dead yet, but he also cannot escape. Realizing this, he chooses to fall to the ground and accept his fate...before he dies. The water buffalo fought as much as he could. In the end, he could not see a way out. It is a slow death as the lions start eating his body before he is dead.

He fought as much as he could, but could not see a way out,
so he chose to lie down and be devoured.

INTUITIVE RESPONSES

Humans are intellectually superior to any other animal on this planet. Because of our intellectual superiority, we are also more unpredictable. We have within us the means to resist surprise attacks because we have studied the natural responses, and unlike the animal kingdom, we have the ability to pass this information to others through personal interactions, books, television, and other media formats. If we use this information to build strong intuitive responses through training then we minimize our innate response. This then moves our reactions to actions. The ability to move quickly using solid foundational intuitive actions assists us in survival.

You have heard the saying "Don't think. Just do." Well, the military has taken this to the next level. Using intensive training, the military preconditions the "do" to be what is known to be the correct re

sponse in a variety of situations. This preconditioning eliminates the need for conscious thought.

It's merely the act of training intuitive responses to be the correct responses. Military members obtain this high state of readiness by training in a dynamic and realistic environment with plausible scenarios. This gives us a solid foundation of experiences from which to draw as we problem-solve on the fly. You may only ever be in one gunfight, but if you have visualized, practiced, trained on a 1000 different dynamic and realistic gunfighting scenarios you more apt to engage the enemy quicker and with more violence thus defeating him. As I have discussed earlier in this book, the need to process information quickly and accurately is paramount as it gives us back that special gift of time. We must utilize existing proven training methods to ensure we get to the *act* portion of the OODA Loop—the decision-making process. Once we *act*. our skills and abilities (honed through training) take center stage.

> *You can't do anything about the bullet with your name on it, but you can do something about the one addressed "To Whom It May Concern."*

SURVIVAL

In a gunfight you have two primary issues—your life and everything else. Your survival is of the utmost concern because you must survive in order to help anyone else. Too often when I talk to women about carrying every day, I am told that they would not use a gun to protect themselves but instead, they would die for their children. My response is a visceral reaction that conveys my disgust for this mentality. I ask them if they want their children growing up in some crappy foster home and being raised by some old hag they don't even know, to which they angrily respond "No!" Then, DON'T DIE! FIGHT! The thought that mothers would protect their children but not themselves is asinine. Look, you have to survive in order to protect others…it's that simple!

> *The mindset is that of ruthless survival, not immortality.*
>
> EJ Owens, Legally Concealed

Upon recognition of a threat we orient ourselves and begin the decision-making process. Here is where realistic training becomes a key component to your survival. What do you do? MOVE! Move from where you are and then keep moving. I don't care if it is to cover at this point. The key is to move.

During training I have my students move during the draw as a way to break the attacker's OODA Loop. Now this is where we start multitasking. You are moving offline of your attacker's threat vector and utilizing the given space to gain a tactical advantage. By moving you are making it harder for the attacker to hit you with the bullet, fist, crowbar, or whatever his choice of weapon happens to be. Speed is important. Movement is *more* important. Once you start your movement you must incorporate your next action, which is to either counter his violence or exit the battle space.

> *Either way, get to doing it, and do so quickly.*

If you are going to return fire, then get your gun up and direct it toward him immediately. Women, if the gun is in your purse, shoot through it. Don't take time to get it out. You can buy a new purse, but not a new life! At intimate distances of five feet or less, simply pointing your gun (or your purse) center mass on his chest and pulling the trigger will do the job. There is no need to squint your non-dominate eye to align your sights. Sight picture happens when you bring the barrel of your gun in line with your nose. Press out and center the gun with the line your nose extending directly in front of you. At five feet or less, this is sufficient to neutralize the attacker. Your training will help you get on target faster.

The faster we kill them, the less they will shoot at us.

When faced with a real deadly threat someone untrained or under-trained most likely will hesitate, probably costing that person his or her life. The untrained or under-trained might fumble when getting his or her gun out of the holster because their draw technique wasn't practiced enough, costing the person to sustain an injury if not lose his or her life. Maybe, the person will crank off a round negligently hitting an innocent bystander because of the mind racing and adrenaline rush that was not expected due to a lack of scenario training. Realistic training will develop solid intuitive shooting stance and draw techniques. Through the repetition of proper training, you will recognize the threat, control your mindset and breathing, draw your weapon and take the kill shot with ease and proficiency.

WYATT PROTOCOL

After moving off line of the threat vector and deciding to draw your gun, it is time to get accurate shots on target and then head for cover. I follow and teach the Wyatt Protocol for Gunfighting—F. A. S. T. It says to...

Fight

Fight, damn it, FIGHT!

Assess

Do I need to fight anymore?

Scan

Do I need to fight anyone else?

Top Off

Prepare to fight again

Once the initial fighting is over you need to determine if the immediate threat is neutralized. You do this by looking around for any other threats that might need to be fought. FBI statistics say that you have over a 50% chance of being attacked by multiple attackers. If so, start fighting them NOW! Once you have determined that there are no more threats and are in a position of cover, reload your gun and get ready for the next fight. Just in case.

ACCURATE SHOTS

Legally and morally we are responsible for all stray rounds. For legal and tactical reasons we want to stop the attacker with as few shots as possible, so our shots need to be accurate. What are *accurate shots?*. Accurate shots are those shots that hit either of two areas vital to life: the brain and the heart.

The skull encloses the brain. The skull is thick bone purposely developed by the body in order to protect this extremely fragile organ. In order to penetrate the brain and stop the attacker, we must place the shots in the cranial ocular cavity that lies behind the eyes and nose. This means that you should aim for the nose. Unless you train often, your body's natural instinct will be to have you hand "kick" (or go up) with the gun as it forces the bullet out of its barrel. If you aim for the eyes and then the gun "goes up", the shot may only glance the at-tacker's head. Shots may also skip off an attacker's skull due to the convex nature of its shape and bone density. Bottom line...aim for the nose.

The human heart is about the size of a closed fist—that is, five to six inches across depend-ing on the angle of meas-urement. The aim point for the heart is high in the chest and center of the nipple line. The spongy bone over the center of your chest is your sternum. It is strong enough to hold your rib cage intact but can also flex to take a blow without cracking. It will not stop a bullet!

You want to ensure that the attacker starts losing blood. As they lose blood, their blood pressure drops. They get light-headed and have trouble thinking. They lose their ability to see clearly. In short, they cease to be a threat. Shooting in the heart stops it. Once the heart stops, so does everything else.

COVER

Seeking cover is one of those things taught as a consideration in shooting schools. Because of the practicality of actually having cover on the range, we rarely integrate it into our live training regiment. We in the gun community talk about seeking cover like it's an implied task—something that we will naturally do. I'm here to tell you that what you do in training is the most you can expect to do in a real gunfight.

You need to put cover between you and the attacker as soon as possible. *Cover* is anything that will stop a bullet. Cover is relative to the weapon being fired at you! It is different than concealment. Concealment is  the attacker not being able to see you, but it doesn't necessarily stop a bullet. We use concealment when we are hunting deer and turkey. If that deer or turkey could shoot back at us, then we would be dead. That's a wild thought I know, but you get my point. Once behind cover look for target indicators like the attacker's shoe, elbow, knee, hip, hands, or maybe a shadow to indicate his location and position. Here is the tip of the day: If you can see it, you can shoot it. However, this goes both ways. When shooting using cover, never come out of cover from the same spot twice in a row. Remember, be unpredictable in order to break the attacker's OODA Loop. Keep him observing while you are acting.

If you are shackled by "fair play," it will likely get you killed!

LEGAL BATTLE

Once you have eliminated the threat and you are safe from any additional threats the next battle is ramping up, the legal battle. I am telling you this for a reason so pay attention because it is vital to your continued walk on this planet. Holster your gun before the police arrive or drop it immediately when they get there. They will not hesitate to shoot you! The last information they received was that someone was shooting up the place and then they see you with a gun in your hands and possibly another person's blood all over you (shooting an attacker up close and personal during a struggle is a bloody mess). They are going to take you into custody. You will get a free pair of steel bracelets to wear during your taxpayer-funded taxi ride to the iron-barred Hilton. You will want to plead your case to convince the officers on the scene of your innocence, but...

SHUT YOUR MOUTH AND ASK FOR A LAWYER!

You don't have to answer any questions. The police on the scene cannot pass judgment and declare you "not guilty"; they are merely note-takers of the event. The decision to press charges falls on the District Attorney (DA). He or she will be briefed on the crime scene findings and the charges that should be considered against you. The DA will then decide what the state will do to you next. In the meantime, you are alive! You survived a heinous act of attempted murder and you came out victorious. You need to understand that our legal system has a process it follows and the process progresses slowly. This will take time to play out. So yes! You were forced into a situation against your will where you had to defend your life from a violent attacker. You survived only to be forced against your will to battle our legal system for your continued freedom. Here is where you need to be at peace with your actions.

EMOTIONAL BATTLE

A clear conscience is of great benefit while you await your outcome. Here is where I rely on my faith to carry me. I know that He guides my path but that I must take responsibility for my own actions. You will go through the following emotions in this order:

Denial

This can't be really happening!

Guilt

Why did I shoot him? Maybe I shouldn't have shot him.

Anger

Why did he make me shoot him?

Depression

I'm a murderer and will have to live with that.

Adjustment

I did what I had to do.

Reconstruction

It happened and I cannot change that. I have to move on.

Acceptance

It's part of me, but it doesn't define me.

This chapter exposes the reality of the burden we bear when carrying a gun for self-protection. It's not sexy nor is it ideal, but it is what survival demands. The acceptance of this burden is the foundation for what we accept when we strap on that burner and roll out into danger zone that is our world. If this burden is too much for you to bear you can always be the African water buffalo and lie down and accept your fate.

We all die. I just want to die on my own terms.

EJ Owens, Founder, Legally Concealed

The fear of death follows from the fear of life.
A man who lives fully is prepared to die at any time.

- Mark Twain

Modern Warrior Certification Program
No B.S. Live Gunfighting Bootcamp

You got what it takes? Apply here:

www.ModernWarrior.org

CHAPTER 9

A Hero's Death

Death teaches us so much about life and about ourselves, even though it can be very difficult to comprehend and experience. As a culture we really don't talk about death, deal with it, or face it in an authentic way. Death often seems too scary, mysterious, personal, loaded, heavy, emotional, tragic, and more.

The thought of death can be detrimental in a gunfight. It can freeze us in a position of cover and panic causing us to lose the advantage of movement. Losing an advantage gives control of our OODA Loop thought process to the attacker. Probably, we die now. So, because of the fear of death, we die without a well-fought fight.

Personally I will not, while there is still a breath left in me, allow these ruthless animals to murder my family or me while I fail to act out of fear for my own safety. I will commit, in the moment, everything that I am to ending the threat to my family and myself. This commitment is sure to become a reality because I can

control my fear. You must learn to control your fear.
Let's talk about that.

COURAGE

There is a fine line separating *fear* from *courage*.
Courage is action is spite of fear. You truly do not know
how you will react in a deadly encounter because we
cannot replicate a training environment that can place
the amount of physiological and emotional duress you
would experience in a real event. You can, however,
learn to control any emotional deviation from your
training that you might experience with a clear and deci-
sive mindset. A mindset of determination and courage
will aid you greatly through "events" but the real key to
survival is to live, live fully with no regrets. Commit
now, this minute, before you continue to read this book
that you will live your life to its fullest.

I have seen death in many of its forms. I have
seen the innocent die. I have seen those who probably
deserved to die slow and painfully, such as the rapist and
child molester ("Deserved" is based on my own moral
and ethical code). While we have all known someone
who has died, most of us separate ourselves from that
experience. We just do not like to think about it. After
all, it is a long way off, right? Sure! So we walk around
on autopilot, caught up in the business—the busyness—of
life. Yet, when we finally believe that we are going to
die, we see things much differently.

I have held the dying in my arms and watched
their souls leave their bodies. Some were undeserving of
death; others well deserved to die. I can tell you this,

though, most of the dying, at the point they recognized that it was their time to go, were filled instantly with regret. Regret is a negative cognitive/emotional state that involves blaming ourselves for a bad outcome. We feel a sense of loss or sorrow at what might have been or wish we could undo a previous choice we made. Interestingly, over short periods of time, people are more likely to regret actions taken and mistakes made, whereas over long periods of time, people are more likely to regret actions not taken, such as missed opportunities for love or working too hard and not spending enough time with family.

Along with their regret is a longing for forgiveness and to forgive. People hurt us intentionally and unintentionally. While we need to correct people who have views that can be divisive and ill informed, it does not mean we need to wipe them out of consciousness. Relationships don't last long if we kill off (figuratively) those who have hurt us. Since relationships give life meaning, we benefit most when we accept the fact that people we love are capable of both good and bad decisions and actions.

EJ's Protocol for a Happy Life

Accept what you are able to do and not able to do.

Accept the past without denying it or discarding it.

Forgive yourself and forgive others.

Never assume it is too late to get involved.

What if we embraced our own death and that of those around us in a vulnerable and genuine way? What if we lived life always aware that we and everyone around us have limited amounts of time here on earth?

Embracing death consciously alters our experience of ourselves, of others and of life in general in a fundamental and transformational way. It allows us to remember what truly matters and to put things in a healthy and empowering perspective. Doing this is much better for us than spending, perhaps wasting our time worrying, complaining, and just surviving the circumstances, situations, and dramas of our lives, isn't it?

The fruit of belief is action, and the benefit of learning how to die physically is to learn how to live spiritually. If faith is part of your life, express it in ways that seem appropriate to you. You may find comfort and hope in reading spiritual texts, attending religious services or praying. Allow yourself to be around people who understand and support your religious beliefs.

When you make the commitment to carry a firearm for self-defense, you are putting the power of life and death within hand's reach. Treat that firearm with the respect it deserves. For today may be the day that death calls you and you must answer. The fear of death is a death sentence. Break free by living.

We should not fear death, but instead,
we should fear not living until death.

Put first things first in your life. Remember, you can't take any of it with you in the end. We all die, and so it doesn't really matter how much you accomplish or how many possessions you accrue. What matters most is the amount of joy you spread, the gratitude you exude and love you cultivate.

MAKE PEACE WITH YOURSELF.
MAKE PEACE WITH YOUR FAMILY.
MAKE PEACE WITH GOD.

Live more consciously each day. Stop sleepwalking through life. Your life is something to be experienced, not coasted through. Escape your ego. Began to see through new eyes. Began a new-found life with friends and a new-found joy with your family and a new-found love in your marriage. Once you have your life in order, then you are able to commit fully in battle. Without hesitation you move, without fear you engage, and without remorse you are victorious. In this moment you don't think twice, there is no need to. You are at peace with yourself and your life. You express your feelings to those you need to, and you have your religious beliefs in order so that should you meet your death on the field of battle you are ready to meet your God.

If I die then I die a free man who loved and lived a wholesome life with no regrets. Those that I leave behind should remember the many things that my life stood for and how I LIVED instead of merely existing. Each day I rise I live that day to the fullest. I pray that when I die, it is in the act of protecting innocence and that through my death, innocence continues to live.

Living without regret, sacrificing your life so that others may live...that is a hero's death. We can only hope that our own death will be worthy of such.

EJ Owens

As I close this chapter, let me share with you this powerful speech that is as much about celebrating life, crossing over, and meeting your maker, as it is about facing the inevitable death of our mortal bodies with grace.

So live your life that the fear of death can never enter your heart.

Trouble no one about their religion; respect others in their view, and demand that they respect yours.

Love your life, perfect your life, beautify all things in your life.

Seek to make your life long and its purpose in the service of your people.

Prepare a noble death song for the day when you go over the great divide.

Always give a word or a sign of salute when meeting or passing a friend, even a stranger, when in a lonely place.

Show respect to all people and grovel to none.

When you arise in the morning give thanks for the food and for the joy of living.

If you see no reason for giving thanks, the fault lies only in yourself.

Abuse no one and no thing, for abuse turns the wise ones to fools and robs the spirit of its vision.

When it comes your time to die, be not like those whose hearts are filled with the fear of death, so that when their time comes they weep and pray for a little more time to live their lives over again in a different way.

Sing your death song and die like a hero going home.

-Tecumseh (1768-1813), Pawnee Chief

You can only fix one thing at a time...so
don't try to solve everything at once.
                                    – A Good Paramedic

**Your FREE Gift Is
Waiting For You Here:**
www.SheepdogSociety.org

CHAPTER 10

Bloody Hands

An intruder has entered into your home and you have grabbed your gun to defend you and your family. As you enter the living room on your way to get the kids to safety you meet the intruder and he is armed! You align your sights just as your youngest daughter runs to your legs screaming. The intruder fires and you fire back hitting him square in the chest. He is down! Thankfully you are not injured but your daughter is lying at your feet with a .380 caliber hole in her chest. The intruder missed you and hit your daughter clinging to your leg. PANIC! Sheer PANIC! She is breathing but it is erratic. You can see her jugular veins bulging out, her chest rise is uneven, and her respirations are now extremely labored. WHAT DO YOU DO?

The average response time for a metro EMS system is 8 to 10 minutes. Because it is the scene of a shooting, the police must "secure the scene" prior to allowing the ambulance and fire truck to pull down. Now your response time is anywhere from 15 to 30 minutes. Your daughter is probably dead by now. As a former firefighter/paramedic for a major metropolitan fire department and a trained U.S. Army medic, I have seen this scenario too many times to count. It is just sad! When there is shooting, somebody is going to bleed. Medical training is a must. God forbid we ever have to defend our homes, but if we do, someone will likely need it—including the attacker.

THERE IS SOMETHING YOU CAN DO!

If you have first responder training and an on-hand trauma kit properly stocked, you can potentially save her life. I want you to understand that you are not helpless. There are skills you can learn and kits you can create or purchase to aid you in this time of need.

TRAINING

First, go to the Red Cross website. Find and complete a CPR/First Aid course taught in your area. Getting certified in CPR/First Aid ensures that you know the basic information for helping either adults or children.

(http://www.redcross.org/takeaclass/programhighlights/cprfirstaid)

The Red Cross CPR/First Aid course provides basic instruction in CPR and wound care. This is the source for your entry into treating life-threatening injuries. They offer both certified and noncertified training options, but choose the certification option. Having that certification card in your wallet increases your confidence that you know the basic information for helping your daughter bleeding to death from a gunshot wound.

American Red Cross

After that, look into getting additional training in emergency medical care. There are companies that offer classes that expand your learning gained in the Red Cross course. The additional training goes deeper into treating trauma, especially airway management for gunshot wounds and stabbings. There are still other companies that provide "on the ground" immediate medical training and I don't want to exclude them. Get some additional training where you can and as soon as you can! Also, any well-respected tactical shooting class should cover trauma treatment to some degree offering you some practical experience to relate to when attending

TRAUMA KIT

A properly stocked, well placed, trauma kit can mean the difference in life or death. There is rarely a situation where just one person is injured so consider putting together several trauma kits. Keep one in your car at all times. Also, keep one upstairs and one downstairs. Put a kit in the garage and consider keeping one at your office. You should always have one in your range bag! You need to keep kits in these locations (at a minimum) because they are probable locations for a conflict.

Also, having several makes it easier to direct someone to retrieve a kit for you.

At a minimum, a trauma kit should include:

1 each	8" x 12" Compression Dressing
1 each	TK4 tourniquet (or SOFTT)
1 each	Gauze bandage roll
1 each	Nasopharyngeal Airway (30fr) Robertazzi Style
2 each	Alcohol Prep Pad
2 each	Safety pin
1 each	Roll of duct tape
1 each	Pair of Nitrile gloves
1 each	Surgilube® Jelly, sterile

Optional, but Recommended:

1 each	14ga 3.25" needle/angiocath
1 each	Chemlite® (red)
1 each	Chemlite® (green)
1 each	Ambu® Bag
1 each	Quickclot®

For recommended medical kits and training go to:

www.LegallyConcealed.org/medical

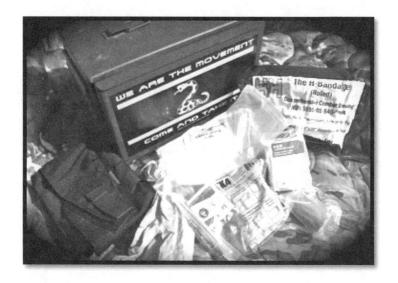

TREATMENT

There are three areas of treatments that you need to become confident handling. Let's go through them.

1. BLEEDING (HEMORRHAGE)

Bleeding must be brought under control quickly because the victim has no way of replacing what is being lost. Bright red blood carrying oxygen to our lungs and thus gives us life. Dark red blood carries deoxygenated blood back to the heart to get oxygenated again. Bright red blood and dark red blood are treated the same way in the field:

- ♥ Direct Pressure (gloved hand)
- ♥ Tourniquet (if applicable)
- ♥ Pressure Bandage

then MORE direct pressure!

2. AIRWAY

It is not uncommon for a wounded patient to pass out due to blood loss because blood loss lowers their blood pressure. When they pass out they can block their own airway. It is imperative that we keep the airway open. We do this by placing a nasopharyngeal airway in

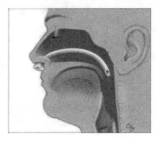

their nose. (This is where the Surgilube comes into play.) You won't get this training in the Red Cross class but you will get it in other "action medical" classes.

The nasopharyngeal tube allows air to get into the lungs upon a respiration when the mouth is closed or affected by trauma. If you don't have a trauma kit handy, then open the airway by turning the patient's head to the uninjured side. Glove your hand. Use your first two fingers to scoop out any debris in his or her mouth that might obstruct good airflow. TIP: If you don't have gloves handy, put your hand in a plastic bag.

3. TENSION PNEUMOTHORAX

A gunshot to the chest is a penetrating wound. There is a danger of air leaving the lung upon respiration and entering the pleural space (essentially the sack containing the lungs). When this happens the lungs cannot expand upon inhalation and the victim suffocates.

We can relieve this by taking a 14ga 3.25" needle and sticking it into the patient's chest providing an escape for the trapped air. Yes, this is pretty high speed and may make you queasy, but being queasy is a hell of a lot better than the feeling you'll get standing beside a casket! Again, you won't get this training in a Red Cross class, but you can get it in most advanced training classes.

While this is a brief explanation on the required training, kit, and treatment to treat victims of some trauma, it should bring to light an area where we all can expand our knowledge. I want you to be prepared for whatever this world throws at you. Handling bleeding and breathing is another skillset you need to have. If you carry a gun then you are carrying a trauma kit...inducing trauma, that is. Ensure that you can be within reach of your other trauma kit...the trauma reducing kit!

I recommend that you make several trauma-reducing kits or purchase prepackaged kits from a reputable source.

A Note From EJ...Buy or put together a trauma kit. Get certified in CPR and First Aid for adults and children. Take additional training classes that focus on bleeding and breathing. Become confident that you can save a life. You might have to save your own some day!

The fight is won or lost far away from witnesses behind the lines, in the gym, and out there on the road, long before I dance under those lights.

-Muhammad Ali

Sheep or Sheepdog
Which One Are You?
Find Out Now. Go To:

www.SheepdogSociety.org

CHAPTER 11

Training

A nyone who thinks that in a real gunfight you are going to handle your firearm as you do when you train on a static range is sadly, even badly, mistaken. Training for a gunfight means acquiring the emotional, mental, and physical skills you need to survive an armed confrontation. Unlike the couple of hours in a concealed carry permit class, successful gunfighting skills require hours of proper training. Once trained, maintenance of those skills requires repetition under realistic and dynamic conditions to induce a reasonable amount of stress to keep those skills sharp and techniques strong.

> *Training Requirements for a Gunfight*
> *Movement*
> *Repetition*
> *Speed*
> *Consistently in Technique*
> *and Stress*

CARRY

Obviously, if you live in a state that requires a permit to carry a firearm out in public then do what it takes to get that. In many states it is a requirement to take a state certified class on firearms as part of the qualification to carry process. These classes, generally speaking, cover the safety rules, basic handling procedures, state laws, and qualifying on a basic course of fire. It is imperative to learn about the laws and the civil liabilities involved in shooting another person to defend yourself and these courses can give you that basic understanding. States all have different requirements as well as differing regulations on where you can and cannot carry. So learning and living by those are of utmost importance.

Gunfighting Rule #1: Bring a Gun!

TRAINING TO FIGHT

If you are new to the shooting community then first start with a good fundamentals of shooting class from a reputable instructor. Depending on your ability and time constraints you may need to take several of these courses and work offline in order to build good technique and instill proper gun handling skills. Once you have the fundamentals down, you are ready to start learning basic and advanced shooting techniques and weapon manipulations that could give you opportunities for survival in a gunfight. There are many good shooting schools across the nation so look for one in your area.

Also, several instructors/schools travel, so don't forget to look for a class that might be hosted near you.

Safety First. You must commit the following safety rules to memory and incorporate them into your everyday life. Teach them to your children, your wife or husband, your friends, significant other, and anyone who will listen!

4 Firearm Safety Rules

1. Treat every gun as if it is loaded.

2. Keep your finger off the trigger until your sights are aligned properly and you are ready to shoot.

3. Never let your muzzle cross anything you are not willing to destroy.

4. Be sure of your target and what's in front and behind it.

Master the Basics. You will need a good foundation of basic marksmanship skills. Advanced shooting skills involve solid applications, and in some cases, modifications of the basic skills. To participate successfully in advance shooting classes, you must first master the basics.

You need good instinctive shooting (also referred to as "*point shooting*" by some instructors). Armed confrontations and gunfights typically happen in seconds. You need to be able to draw (most likely from concealment) and shoot multiple targets accurately. Then, you need to be able to do this as fast as possible.

<u>Gunfighting Training Rule #1</u>
Accuracy first, then speed!

You need good shooting from retention skills. Most gunfights happen at close distances and you will more than likely be fighting one or more assailants coming toward you. You will need to hold onto your gun tightly while firing multiple accurate shots.

You have to move! You're going to move. One way or another, you are going to move! Hopefully, you are moving offline of the attack and not down to the ground because you took a heat round. You need to incorporate movement into your training! A person who stays still is an easy target, and in fact, may end up lying still in a box. Conversely, the person who moves rapidly is more likely to survive the fight.

<u>Gunfighting Training Rule #2</u>
Move while practicing because that is most likely what you will do in a real gunfight!

INSTRUCTORS

Seek out instructors from both the competition world and those who have been involved in real world action. My mother has a saying that has stuck with me all my life-"take the good and leave the bad". With all the classes that you are sure to take, there will undoubtedly be tactics and skill-based techniques that just don't work for you. That's ok! Take what does work for you and leave the other in your toolbox for later consideration or as a conversation piece on poker night. Select tactics, techniques and equipment that work for you, but pay special attention to the proven combat techniques from both the military and tactical law enforcement applications. Remember, it doesn't have to be sexy. It just has to work.

PHYSICAL FITNESS

Beyond shooting, physical fitness is also critical to survival. The better shape you are in, the faster you can move and the less likely you are to get hurt. I watch too many individuals rely on their weapon and ancillary "Gucci Gear" to solve all the problems. The issue with this is that you have to move that weapon into a solid shooting position not once, but multiple times during an engagement. This requires strength, stamina and endurance. Many folks do not have the physical conditioning to get to or stay in the fight. That next area of cover may seem like 10 miles away if you are out of shape. Also, think about this...your physical fitness level maybe the determining factor as to whether you can keep your loved ones safe when the lead starts flying.

REALISTIC TRAINING

I hammer home the use of cover to all my students. Brick walls and dirt stop bullets better than your house walls and car, believe it or not. Many of the competitions that I have watched or participated in have the shooter exposed to multiple targets during the course of fire. This is okay for the game, but if you overexpose yourself to multiple opponents, they can all shoot at you.

If they are shooting at you, then you are probably seeking cover rather than shooting back. Learn to engage and expose yourself to one threat at a time. Make the bad guy give you a full body shot to engage while you only give him your shooting eye and weapon. Don't get caught flatfooted in the open. In short, make yourself a hard target.

Gunfighting Training Rule #3

Maximize the use of cover, minimize your exposure.

Realistic tactical training may not feel rewarding at first. There are no prizes, certificates, or trophies to be had. The reward is being able to solve a deadly problem quickly and efficiently in your immediate space. The other reward is being able to go home at the end of the day, give the spouse a kiss and put the kids to bed.

SHOOTING OR A GUNFIGHT

A *shooting* is one-way event. You do all the shooting! A *gunfight* is a two-way (or more) event. You do some of the shooting while someone shoots, too. The difference between a gunfight and a competition is that the other shooter is shooting you—not at a paper target or a can on a fence.

Gunfights may lead to your getting shot and that is going to hurt! A lot! How do you make a "gunfight" into a "shooting"? Simple! See the threat faster, anticipate the next moves in the fight, and react more quickly than the other shooter.

Realistic training will put you in more "probable" scenarios to help you think faster and more tactically sound, should you actually be in a real gunfight. Your survival begins by setting yourself up in a tactically superior position before the fight happens. Control your opponent's O.O.D.A. loop and dominate the fight. Additionally, equipment, physical fitness and overall mindset play critical roles in your success.

UP CLOSE TARGETS

As for shooting and closing on a target, it only makes the bad guy's accuracy better. Walking into a muzzle may help you to test your newly found Superman powers sooner than you wished. Angled movement works, but again if you have to slow down too much, you are an easy target, and are generally in the open. Speed can act as your security in this case to get you to a point of cover.

LONG RANGE TARGETS

Shooting at longer ranges helps establish proper sight alignment and trigger control. You have to take your time to line the shot up in order to hit the target. Once you can hit long range targets (25+ yds.), you will see the front sight and the target area at closer ranges much clearer and your accuracy will improve.

All too often, I see instructors relying on some FBI statistic saying that the majority of gunfights take place at closer distances, therefore they only train at closer distances. I would ask you to think about an active shooter situation where some scumbag has started shooting up a mall and he is across the food court from you. Can you hit him from where you are? Probably not! You have to train for it.

SHOOTING ON THE MOVE

Shooting on the move is a skill that all shooters aspire to learn and spend a great deal of time and effort trying to master. When moving at a careful hurry, you will still find yourself stopping to plant your feet in order to make the shots. When the bullets are flying, sprinting from cover to cover is moving too fast to shoot. There is no in between. If you slow down enough to make a solid hit when under fire, you are an easy target. So, you have to make your decisions wisely. This is where Hollywood misleads you. They show slow-motion scenes of our hero advancing under a hail of bullets all the while making accurate shots and not getting hit. That's crap! You have to move quickly under fire. PERIOD! Get to cover then select your targets carefully and make accurate hits. Also, let me remind you that you do not have unlimited ammo like in Call of Duty. You will eventually run out so make your shots count.

A Note From EJ:

All of your training should be helping you to prepare mentally for sudden attacks and shooting under pressure. If you are not failing in your training drills then you are not pushing yourself hard enough. Amateurs practice till they get it right; professionals practice till they get it wrong. Master the basics and then work your way through the advanced skills keeping in mind: Accuracy first and then speed.

Excellence is an art won by training and habitation.
We do not act rightly because we have virtue or
excellence, but we rather have those because we have
acted rightly. We are what we repeatedly do.
Excellence, then, is not an act but a habit."

- Aristotle

In a real life or death scenario you will not, "rise to the occasion."

You will only perform at the level you've trained for.

If you want serious, tactical firearms training, I invite you to apply for the Modern Warrior Certification Program. Limited availability. Apply now:

www.ModernWarrior.org

MODERN WARRIOR

CHAPTER 12

Preparing To Attend A Shooting Class

A ll too often shooting classes are held up because that "someone" just isn't ready yet. That "someone" is still loading magazines (*mags*), still unboxing ammo, or because they just can find something. I have seen it all and I want to help you not be that "someone"! Here are the things you need to do during your preparation time, prior to attending a shooting class, so that you're keeping with the pace of the class and maximizing your learning potential. You paid good money to be there so let's keep you on the shooting line.

WHAT YOU NEED

EVERYDAY CARRY PISTOL

First things first. You should train with the gun you are going to carry! All too often I see people using a Glock 17 (full size 9mm) for the class only to put it away at the end of the training day and strap on a Glock 26

(subcompact 9mm). This is not doing you any good. If it is not what you are going to carry on an everyday basis then don't train with it. Now, let me qual-

ify this, if you are proficient on your everyday carry gun and are attending a course to become proficient on another gun, then it is fine to train on something besides your everyday carry.

Be absolutely sure you are good to go with your everyday carry first! If you carry a back-up gun as part of your everyday carry then wear and train with it too. What a great time to run that gun! Just let your instructor know before class starts that you want to use it and make sure they are okay with it. This won't be a problem with most instructors.

SPARE GUN

I recommend you bring a spare gun to train with should your everyday carry gun go down hard. I have

seen it happen several times. Luckily, the instructor let the person use his personal weapon or the range had rentals to use. Nothing can hurt your experience more than your smoke wagon taking a crap on you in the middle of Day One.

Food for thought! You should also bring spare parts for your gun. If you don't have the knowledge and/or skill to replace it, don't worry. There are always people there that can help you and/or your instructor should be able to get one of his guys to fix it for you while you use your spare. Again, this helps with your experience by keeping you on the shooting line.

RIFLE

When you attend a rifle course you should bring the rifle you are most likely to use in a personal defense situation. Your rifle should be zeroed prior to attending  and that means the iron sights and co-witnessing the optic. Also, your pistol and rifle should come to class clean and well lubricated. All screws should have a drop of the medium grade Loctite® on them. Remember, you are going to run these guns hard and the vibration from the recoil will eventually loosen the screws. Then high dollar items tend to give way to Earth's gravitational pull.

MAGAZINES

The more magazines (mags) you bring, the longer you stay on the line. Don't just bring the two or three mags the gun came with. Most stoppages occur from bad mags. I recommend you bring at least six pistol and ten rifle mags depending on the course you are attending. This goes for your back up and spare as well if they take different ones than your primary. Prior to class all of your mags should be loaded.

I have never seen an instructor get upset because one of his students had to unload. If, however, you show up without having mags already loaded you have set yourself apart as that "someone" without ever stepping up on the shooting line.

AMMO

When attending a shooting class bring good quality ammo. Wolf Ammo for AK types and PMC or Federal bulk for AR's are always good choices. For pistol ammo you have a lot of choices but if you are running a 1911 then use the ammo that YOU know will run without problems. Take all the ammo out of its packaging and dump them into an ammo can or box. Nothing irritates an instructor more, outside of a safety violation, than watching that "someone" open boxes of ammo and

load mags.

So do everyone at the class and yourself a favor and just bring an ammo can full of loose ammo. If your buddies want to grab one of your mags and help you load then they just reach in your ammo can and grab a handful of ammo. This really speeds up the process of getting back up on the shooting line. If you need a little extra help in loading or you just want to save your fingers then purchase and bring with you a Tula loader. *(You can thank me later!)*

CLEANING KIT

Bring a well-stocked cleaning kit and extra lubrication and grease. The cleaning kit you might not need to use but if you don't bring it you WILL need it. The lubricant should be easy to apply and readily available. Also, just as important, bring a multi-tool or a tool kit with Allen wrenches. Things come loose and you will need tools to tighten them back up. If you are using an optic that requires a special tool (i.e. Aimpoint Micro), make sure that it travels with you to the range every day of class. Bring extra batteries for your optic too! Murphy is hitching a ride with you to class and he decides when he wants to play, so be prepared.

EYE AND EAR PROTECTION

Eye and ear protection are a must. If you are using eye pro that has tinted lens then bring the clear ones too. A small cleaning rag is a good idea because they are going to get dirty from sweat and dust. I highly recommend electronic hearing protection like Comp-Tac's® because you are going to find it hard to hear if you are down on the end of the shooting line. Instructors tend hang out near the middle of the line and you will struggle to hear if you bring the ear muffs your dad gave you to cut the lawn with. When you bring electronic hearing protection bring extra batteries for them too! Remember, Murphy hitched a ride with you!

MEDICAL

As with every trip to the range you should bring a first aid kit (Band-Aids®, ointment, etc.) and a trauma kit (gunshot blowout kit). The trauma kit should have at least a pressure bandage and tourniquet in it. This way, if you get shot or shoot yourself, there is something to treat you with until the ambulance arrives. I pray that never happens to you but...better prepared than dead.

EXTRAS

Your holster, belt, and extra mag carrier should be the same one you are using in your everyday carry. Showing up in the latest Call of Duty (CoD) gear has no practical purpose if that is not your duty gear, yet there will be several that show up looking like they are CoD Prestige Level 4. I've seen it time and time again. You will see a desk jockey by day and a DeltaSEALRanger Command Private Major in class. Okay, go ahead and laugh. It is a funny thought and even funnier in real life. I chuckle to myself every time one of those guys waltzes into class! Regardless of what you bring make sure to test fit it all and simulate movements you will perform in class. Make any necessary adjustments before you leave home.

Go ahead and pack everything the packing list says to bring because the instructor has a good reason why it's on there, so don't question it. The weather has a way of changing when you are stepping onto the shooting line and it pays to be prepared. If the packing list doesn't say to bring sunscreen and bug spray, bring it anyway. Mother Nature is queen and you could become her court jester if you don't. Dehydration and fatigue are ever present. Bring a cooler full of ice and bottled water. Bring snack foods. Power bars, granola, and some candy for sugar are good choices. Go ahead and purchase a case of bottled water. Throw it in your vehicle to resupply your cooler throughout the course.

Prepare yourself for the class. Get in the best possible shape you can in the time you have before the

class starts. You want to be able to complete all the drills without hurting yourself. Also, bring knee pads and elbow pads. You may not need them, but then again, you might just save those $200 Kryptek® pants you bought.

As I do with every gun owner I meet I am recommending that you read Colonel Jeff Cooper's book *Principals of Personal Defense*. It is the ultimate authority on the defensive mindset. You can read it in about an hour or less. It is life changing!

Now get out there and go train!

Few men are born brave.
Many become so through training and force of discipline.

-*Publius Flavius Vegetius Renatus*

SHEEP: people who depend on others to protect and take care of them.

SHEEPDOGS: those who are willing to face evil and defend themselves and the flock.

Which one are you? Find out here:

www.SheepdogSociety.org

Closing

Starting in Genesis when Cain killed Able violence has been a part of our lives. It haunts millions of families that have lost loved ones due to it. We can't escape our very nature. We can, however, defend ourselves from such violence by harnessing the intelligent animalistic nature that lies inside each and every  one of us. We are capable of counter-violence if the will is there. Violent attackers believe you won't fight back. Instead, they expect you to lie down and beg for your life as they ruthlessly take it away from you. You have people who depend on you, that need you, so you have to live. Your kids need their father and mother, your spouse needs you to care and comfort him or her. To let some animal take your life before your walk on this planet is over is senseless.

> *FIGHT! Fight for your sake. Fight for their sakes.*
>
> *FIGHT, FIGHT, FIGHT and LIVE!*

The animals that would put you in a position of defending your life and the lives of your family care nothing of your family's needs for you. They want what they want and don't care how they get it. If you have the mindset, skill, and tactics, you have a fighting chance at surviving a deadly encounter and with proper training you can obtain it. It is imperative that you meet violence with counter-violence, and that you finish it!

Frederick the Great had a saying that General Patton loved to repeat to his troops, *"Audacity, audacity, always audacity!"* You have to be audacious and aggressive toward the criminal. Some may say that audacious and aggressive are not in their character, but without them, these people (now victims) will likely be dead. You...well, you will live...live to see your daughter or son celebrate another birthday or perhaps walk down the aisle at their wedding. Please take to heart the subjects discussed in this book, as they are what my military and professional training, my education, my personal experi-

ences, and my faith tell me are needed to survive.

MAY GOD BLESS AND PROTECT YOU!

-EJ Owens

Appendix A

STATES WITH CASTLE DOCTRINE
LEGISLATION ENACTED IN 2012

Alaska	Tennessee
Arizona	Mississippi
Idaho	Alabama
Montana	Georgia
Wyoming	Florida
North Dakota	South Carolina
South Dakota	Kentucky
Nebraska	Indiana
Oklahoma	Ohio
Texas	West Virginia
Missouri	Michigan
Louisiana	Maine

Reference:

http://www.concealandcarryhq.com/

"Warriors Aren't Born. They're Made."

We Offer Real-World, Live Training Events.
For Info Go To:

www.ModernWarrior.org

ABOUT THE AUTHOR

EJ Owens is a firearms instructor specializing in concealed carry and home defense scenarios. EJ is a Close Quarters Battle (CQB) instructor and a U.S. Army Hand-to-Hand Combat instructor. As a former Infantry Officer, he is a veteran of the U.S. Army and National Guard.

Active in church and civic organizations, EJ brings his expertise as a former firefighter/NREMT-P paramedic with specialties in Nuclear-Bio–Chemical Response to each event. EJ is a Certified Glock Armorer, Rope Rappel Master, and a Competitive IDPA Shooter. He holds a M.B.A. in Organizational Management. EJ is the founder and president of Legally Concealed. He lives in Memphis, Tennessee with his wife, Jennifer and his three children, Kaleb, Olivia, and Ethan.

Please check out EJ's other projects including:

Become a member of the Sheepdog Society today!
For all the details and to claim your free gift, visit:

www.SheepdogSociety.org

Live Training Events
For info about our **Modern Warrior Certification Program** and live training events visit:

www.ModernWarrior.org

Training Courses
For our latest training courses including **Tactical Home Defense** and **Everyday Carry** please visit:

www.LegallyConcealed.org

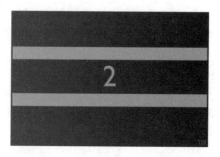

STAY ALERT AND PRACTICE OFTEN! ™

Email EJ at ejowens@legallyconcealed.org.